Keeping On

www.mascotbooks.com

Keeping On

I have tried to recreate events, locales, and conversations from my memories of them.
In order to maintain their anonymity, in some instances I have changed the names
of individuals and places. I may have changed some identifying characteristics and
details such as physical properties, occupations, and places of residence.

Cover photograph by Greg Ellison, reporter, *Ocean City Today*

For more information, please contact:
Mascot Books
620 Herndon Parkway, Suite 320
Herndon, VA 20170
info@mascotbooks.com

Library of Congress Control Number: 2020907769

CPSIA Code: PRV0720A
ISBN: 978-1-64543-350-7

Printed in the United States

This book is dedicated to three individuals who taught me
everything I know about keeping on,
even in the face of adversity:
my mother, Cecilia Kernan Staub;
my husband, Ernie Hoskins;
and
my teacher, Sister Catherine Cesnik.

Keeping On

How I Came to Know
Why I Was Born

Gemma Hoskins

From the Emmy-nominated
NETFLIX docuseries *The Keepers*

Contents

PROLOGUE

The Second Most Important Day

I don't drive. I know, right? When I first began to use Uber, I was lucky to find a driver I could schedule ahead of time. She even let my dog ride in her car so we could get to the vet. When *The Keepers* was released, she knew who I was. She is a good and caring person, and sort of fascinated that people look at me curiously. The months after the series aired were not easy for me (more about that later), but "Uber Philis" has always been consistent and kind, prompt and respectful, humble and funny, down-to-earth. And proud that she is "driving Miss Gemma."

One day when Philis picked me up, I was stressed about trying to keep a modicum of normalcy in my life without losing my focus on Sister Cathy and the abuse survivors. I unloaded. She listened. Pulling into True Value Hardware, Philis said something I'll never forget: "I don't know where I heard this, but did you know there are two important days in your life?"

"Is this a riddle? What are they?" I asked.

"The first important day is the day you were born, right? And the second most important day is the day you figure out why."

Keeping On is like peeling an onion. The face I have presented to the world most of my life has not always been authentic, but this memoir reveals my still-developing true self. I hope I get there, but do we ever? The murder of my teacher and why she was killed is also, in part, a story about why I think I was born. It's about why I am searching for answers to what happened fifty years ago. This book is about understanding why and how events, good and bad, brought me to the realization that the work I am doing is the reason I was born. My feeling different is still there; it's often surreal. But I am going to share with you that my journey to find Cathy's murderer and to advocate for survivors of abuse by clergy is fueled by what I have learned jumping over hurdles and moving forward, often alone.

This is not going to be an easy tale to tell. I have put it off a long time. It is going to mean poking my finger into some painful experiences. But I want you, the reader, to know that I am committed to rocking boats for those who can't do it themselves. My very large personality, my loud voice and my bold writing might get on your nerves. You will want to tell me to settle down, chill, take a break, back off, be gentler, and take care of myself. You are going to hear about things I have never told anybody.

For this effort, I am going to be trolled and trashed and criticized. It won't be the first time. I'm really working on not worrying about what people think of me—I want a thicker skin. But neither has happened yet, so don't hold your breath. Don't get me wrong: I have a very healthy ego and a lot of confidence in what I am doing. However, I am afraid to say that I like to be recognized for things I have done well. Every time somebody tells me what a great job I have done with all things "Keepers," my response is, "Thanks, but it is always a team effort." But it's not always a team effort. Keeping on is not hard for me, but it is hard saying that I have done a lot of the moving and shaking of the church and other institutions on my own. Maybe I tell myself that I am not alone because I am afraid for my personal safety and there is safety in numbers, but I do not really believe that. When I walk down the street with my dog, I do seriously consider that somebody in a slowing car could very well shoot me in the back of the head. I just hope if that happens, it will be fast and I will not suffer.

So, you are going to learn how shy and insecure and vulnerable I am. And how much I need your acceptance and approval, and for you to keep telling me I am a badass and "you go, girl." I need to know that you are praying, or yoga-ing, or doing whatever you do to send me positive energy. And know that I am going to do the same for you.

A chance connection with journalist Tom Nugent (who you'll meet in this story right away), set me on a journey of questions and discovery, probing and not finding. But I had been down such a road before. My whole life, I realized, was one of endless questions, unforeseen events and challenges. I had learned early to develop strategies and resources in order to move on through joy and heartache. My journey through uncharted territory was replicated as I began to search for who killed Sister Cathy.

PART ONE

Who Killed Sister Cathy?

1

Questions

Journalist Tom Nugent found me by chance in 2004. Contributing to his writing about Sister Cathy Cesnik was an honor. Then an obsession. Then an addiction. I made up my mind to use my talents and contacts to find out what had happened to my favorite teacher, murdered at the age of twenty-six for knowing too much. She gave her life for those she loved.

Who killed Sister Cathy? This is a question I and many of you have asked every day now for years. I think I can answer it, but in the world of cold-case homicides, there are only three ways to solve this fifty-year-old mystery: a confession, an eyewitness, or DNA. Right now, all three are possible but none are likely. I believe, however, there is enough circumstantial evidence that points to what happened to my teacher on November 7, 1969. Come with me and I will tell you.

Early in 2004, on a Sunday afternoon, I was at my usual spot in the basement workroom of my Temple Hills townhome in Bel Air, Maryland (yeah, the homes near the Wheel Road snowball stand). As a teacher mentor for Baltimore County Public Schools, I was preparing for my week by creating demonstration lesson plans to be delivered to my teachers at Lansdowne Middle School. A supervisor with whom I once worked, Robert Christopher, always told me that if a teacher was formally observed unexpectedly, a few hiccups were acceptable, but if a teacher knew there would be an observation, the lesson needed to be stellar. In my work as a mentor, I took that advice to heart. If I was demonstrating a strategy or new content for a novice or struggling teacher, I knew that my written plan and its delivery needed to be perfect: new teachers would see my errors immediately. Building their trust also meant delivering the goods they needed and wanted. Deep into lesson objectives and assessment, I was distracted by the ringing of my landline.

The gentleman on the other end of the call introduced himself as Tom Nugent. Nugent explained that he had been in Baltimore and had visited my old high school, Archbishop Keough. While there, he was able to borrow copies of yearbooks and lists of alumnae. Now Tom was toiling through the arduous task of locating former students. His purpose, he told me, was to find Keough students who had known an English and drama teacher, Sister Catherine Cesnik. Immediately, my thoughts went to the days I spent in her class-room or on the stage as a performer in the drama club. And then, of course, to her terrible death in November 1969, at the hands of a still unknown perpetrator. I had never heard of Tom Nugent, but as we talked, I realized that he was very determined to shed light not only on Cathy's death but also her life and the impact she had on those who knew her. I was honored to tell Tom that Cathy was the reason I became a teacher and that, as a teacher, I utilized many of the strategies she used in her classroom at Keough. He encouraged me to talk about her dynamic Julie Andrews personality, her love for literature and drama, her care for her students.

Working with Tom on this story, and providing contact information for some of my classmates, I began to have more questions. What really happened to Cathy? Did some guy kill her while she was out shopping? Now, there were rumors that some of my classmates had been raped by the nerdy priest who said Mass and heard confessions at Keough. My younger sister, Maria, and I had both attended Keough. How could we have missed something like rape? There would have been screaming and police officers and chaos in the halls. A priest? *That* priest? It couldn't be true. Or could it? I only remembered receiving a letter from a lawyer in the early 1990s asking if anybody knew anything about sexual abuse at the school. Now it was being connected to Sister's death.

Wow.

When Tom Nugent finished writing his story—"Who Killed Sister Cathy?"—he sent it to me for my perusal. I thought it was powerful, frightening, and would raise many more questions for those who read it. Because Tom had worked for years as an investigative reporter at the *Baltimore Sunpapers*, we both figured that it would want to publish such an eye-opening news story. After a lot of back and forth with editors and his friends at the *Sun*, the paper decided the story had too many loose ends, too many unanswered questions. Tom told me that the *Sun* claimed that there could be legal ramifications if the paper printed the story. What was going on? Why were they afraid of this story? Tom then moved on to the *Washington Post*. Then the *New York Times*. Same response. No thanks, Mr. Nugent. Your story is too volatile. Too explosive. Finally, thanks to Nugent's persistence, the liberal *Baltimore City Paper* agreed to publish "Who Killed Sister Cathy?" Although the *City Paper* is now defunct, its courageous and bold role in publishing this bombshell gives it kudos.

Nugent told me that if the *City Paper* had said no, he was going to print thousands of copies of the story himself and walk around Baltimore handing them out. I probably would have done that with him. My kind of person, Tom was. (You see Tom in his attic in the first few moments of *The Keepers* with that huge story weighing heavily on his lap. Very heavily.)

Thus began my obsession with this very cold case.

In 2006, "Who Killed Sister Cathy?" ruffled some feathers. Tom's fearless and articulate writing gave new life to this cold case. He proposed that Cathy had been murdered because she was aware that the school chaplain, Reverend Joseph Maskell, was a pedophile. Perhaps she had reported him to her superiors or to the police. But things settled down, and we all continued to wonder. One day in 2010, I sent Tom an email.

Fri, Aug 13, 2010 12:20 am

ghoskins

Are you the Tom Nugent who wrote the article about Sister Catherine? We discussed it on the phone several times. If you are, let me know. For some reason, it is bugging the hell out of me, like it could still be solved.

Gemma Staub Hoskins

And then this one two years later:

Tue, Nov 27, 2012

Hi Tom

You interviewed me several years ago for this article which appeared in the Baltimore City Paper—apparently there was an article in the Baltimore Sun on Sunday about the case—I am wondering if you ever heard any more about it from your research - sure would make a great movie. Do you remember me?

Gemma Hoskins
Keough 1970

PS. Are you on Facebook?

And then this one:

Fri, Aug 2, 2013 12:23 am

Tom,

Have just reread your Sister Cathy story from 2005 and it still gives me the creeps. Anyway, I want to know if you are really going to return to this story, which is losing its players fast. I bet we could solve it.

Cheers
Nancy Drew
(Gemma Hoskins)

And then from Tom:

> Hello again Gemma. I'm still determined to work on the story again—I will return to Balt in Sept—if you want to work on it that would be very helpful—I will create a website where any and all players can file info, newspaper clips, personal memories etc—will do that by Labor Day—let's plan to meet in Sept in Balt to discuss?
>
> Best,
> Tom Nugent

Tom suggested I post a message on the Keough alumnae page asking if anybody who knew anything about Sister Cathy, or had information about Joseph Maskell, would be willing to talk to him. I was happy to oblige, but in doing so, all hell broke loose. I was reprimanded by a moderator of the alumnae page who said this was not an appropriate topic. The page, I was told, was reserved for news of reunions, babies, weddings, success stories, sports accomplishments. Not abuse or murder. *What the hell?* I thought. I shortly got bumped off that page.

I appealed to a close Keough friend, Margaret Phelan, who lived in Chicago to go to bat online for me. With her gentle but firm intercession, eventually I was admitted back onto the alumnae page. But I quickly bailed because I could see that, indeed, it was certainly not the arena in which to explore abuse and murder. However, two tech savvy Keough women, Laurie Rollins and Janine Heiner, whom I have still never met, quickly set up a page for the discussion, and that was the beginning of a safe place for Keough abuse survivors and their supporters to share. The page became known as AKHS Survivors. It remains, to this day, that very same safe place. Only Keough alumnae are admitted, and they must be known by at least two others on the page. Abbie Schaub does a yeoman's job of keeping everybody safe and informed.

My next error was to ask on that new page whether anybody had information about Cathy's murder. Foot in mouth again. I was told this was not a witch hunt, so I retreated with my computer mouse into silence, but not for long. Again, Laurie and Janine saved me with a new and public Facebook page named "Justice for Catherine Cesnik and Joyce Malecki." Joyce was another local young woman who had been murdered shortly after Cathy disappeared. I quickly became known as a boat rocker. But in a good way, of course. That page thrived for several years but went belly-up with a traffic jam when *The Keepers* was released. (It does still exist as a sort of announcement site.)

As the AKHS Survivors page grew, so did our responsibilities. Putting survivors of abuse by Joseph Maskell in touch with Tom Nugent was a careful, consistent procedure. As women expressed to me an interest in talking to Tom about what had happened to them at Keough, I would, with their permission, share their contact information with him. Tom would then send an introductory email to each woman, copying me in each email sent, since we agreed that the women would be more comfortable if I stayed in the loop. Until they indicated to us that they would like to talk by phone or in person with Tom, I remained in that chaperone role. All were reassured that their names and information would remain confidential.

As the months went by, many survivors shared their stories of horrific abuse with me and Tom. Most have gone public, and you met them in *The Keepers*. Interestingly, many of these women knew each other at Keough, but none had shared what happened to them with each other. Sitting together on the bus, walking to class, hanging out in the gym or lounge, these girls were threatened into silence.

Some had repressed some of their memories, so their stories were in fragments. As time has gone by, with the help of therapists and each other, a lot of Maskell survivors have remembered their abuse and have begun the healing process.

The Justice for Catherine Cesnik and Joyce Malecki Facebook page was a horse of a different color. This was a public page, and it grew quickly. Word spread fast, and as administrators, Abbie (with whom I had attended Keough but had not been personal friends) and I, and a few other Keough friends, facilitated, clarified, documented and dug. Abbie became the constant voice of reason on these pages. I had more emotional reactions to the issues at hand. Abbie would often advise that we all take a step back and look at the facts and rumors objectively and judiciously. We became partners in crime detection.

Collaborating from our homes via our computers and phones, a bigger picture began to emerge from what many people were telling us. A picture that this murder was way more insidious than we had thought: the abuse was not restricted to Maskell but included other individuals. The network of perpetrators appeared to be a widespread ring of drugs, mind control, torture, and prostitution. The list of accused individuals included high-ranking politicians, police officers, other clergy, businesspersons, thugs. And lots of money had changed hands. As this picture developed, other trusted friends offered to help us. Unfortunately, some of them were false friends and have either disappeared or turned against us. Others have come to be faithful and supportive participants. *Our tribe.*

Late one evening, I was reading posts on the Justice page when a woman sent me a private message. She believed her uncle had killed Sister Cathy. My mouth flew open. So much for sleep that night. A few minutes later, I was on the phone with Debbie Yohn, the niece of a man named Edgar Davidson. I learned from Debbie that, as a very young child, she accompanied Davidson on his drives around Baltimore while he attempted to pick up young girls. Her information continued to be invaluable as we learned that he was likely working with Joseph Maskell to recruit girls to be drugged and prostituted. Debbie became an integral part of our ensuing investigation. She tried relentlessly, as did the rest of Davidson's family, to convince him to do the right thing. Debbie's background in nursing and her role speaking to teens about making good decisions about drugs and alcohol, have served her well in her ongoing work as an advocate for survivors and a very active member of the Survivors Network of those Abused by Priests (SNAP).

Shortly after, we realized that our grassroots investigation was picking up speed. Abbie's techno-wizard daughter, Kate, assisted us by setting up a tip line so that readers could submit anonymous information to us. This provided an avenue to many individuals, especially locally, who remembered something, or had an article, or knew an ex-cop, or had a connection to a parish or school. One day, a message came across the tip line from another woman who told us that she believed her uncle, who had been Cathy's neighbor, was involved in her murder. Thus we met Sharon Schmidt.

Her story was similar in some ways to that of Debbie Yohn, but the women did not know each other, and their uncles had no connection we could find. But these two pieces of information were shared willingly by the women with the police. Debbie had informed the police of her suspicions years before and was even outfitted with a hidden microphone by the police department in order to record a meeting with her Uncle Ed at a restaurant. Problems with the mike, and Edgar's suspicion that he was being watched, meant the interaction was unproductive. However, Debbie continued to share whatever information she and her family had that would help. I think it took the Schmidt family also coming forward for the police to take another look at the case.

When we started our own investigation into the murder of Cathy Cesnik, we were not welcomed by the cold-case police department or the local FBI. The detective responsible for Cathy's case at the time, was polite but suggested we spend our time on other hobbies. He was dismissive of our offers of help, reassuring us there was never any evidence that any religious persons were involved in the murder. We were given the impression that he considered us little old ladies in the community, stirring up a lot of trouble. Little did he know, until we accompanied Cathy's sister Marilyn to the police station, that neither of us was anywhere near ready for the grave. In fact, we could probably have taken him down . . . well, maybe not.

The local FBI office was also disinterested in what we were doing. Tom Nugent visited that office to offer information but was rudely told to get out. I invited that agent to join our Facebook page. How naive of me to think that he would! But I bet those guys are kicking themselves right now. Our Facebook members were on board with us. Everybody wanted answers.

In September 2013, I received a call from a young woman who worked as a writer for the *Huffington Post*. She had been reading our posts because her area of interest was women's issues and rights. Laura Bassett soon became a trusted friend, visiting Baltimore regularly to accompany us as we dug for information. Laura attended our meetings, took a tour of the areas where Cathy taught, lived and died. The result of her six-month journey with us was an earthshaking story titled "Buried in Baltimore: The Mysterious Murder of a Nun Who Knew Too Much."

We owe Laura a great deal for her very caring and perceptive coverage of the story that was unfolding. At the same time, though, our work was reaching media outlets that were not interested in finding the answers but in the sensationalism of the story of a nun with a boyfriend who left the convent and was murdered. Abbie and I made a firm agreement that we would say no to any of those outlets that were going to sensationalize an already salacious and horrible tale. We resolved that we would never agree to do anything publicly or privately that would hurt anyone or retraumatize anyone who had already suffered so much.

2

The Keepers

We were into the second year of this investigation, most of which was done on the internet and social media, when Tripod Media, the filmmakers responsible for *The Keepers,* found me. They had already made numerous trips from Los Angeles to Baltimore, meeting with Jean Wehner ("Jane Doe" in *The Keepers*) and her family. Unless Jean was comfortable committing to a docuseries, director Ryan White and producer Jessica (Lawson) Hargrave would not have reached out to me. A phone call from Jessica in November 2014 was the start of my relationship and collaboration with Tripod Media, which presented me with an opportunity to tell the story of my investigation. After a two-hour phone call with Jessica and very little consideration, I agreed to meet with the filmmakers.

A few weeks later, we arranged to meet in the parking lot of the local Home Depot. Coincidentally, the house where I was living in Relay, Maryland, was in the exact center of all the events surrounding Sister Cathy's death and the abuse connected with it. My new friend and survivor, Teresa Lancaster ("Jane Roe" in *The Keepers*) accompanied us. I remember bringing Teresa a package of candy with the label Lancaster (I had no idea how this was going to go but figured candy always helps). Up rolled our new friends. Jessica was a tiny adorable blonde waif, while Ryan was a tall and swarthy dude. They looked to be about eighteen. They told us they had been best friends all their lives.

After introductions, they climbed into my old red Jeep Liberty. We were about to take what I have irreverently referred to as the ghost tour. Our first stop was the circular driveway at Archbishop Keough High School. Approaching the concrete latticework across the front of the building, Teresa pointed out the fire door, through which Maskell admitted men, and where he let her stand outside, unseen, to have a cigarette. Of course, a teacher immediately saw us and asked us what we wanted. We were ready for this. We were alumnae who were showing our friends from California the school, because they were interested in enrolling their young daughter in the Catholic elementary school, which now was on the first floor of the building. About forty high school students attended classes on the second floor. At the peak of its popularity, Keough students numbered twelve hundred. Fifty years later, the economy, and other factors, heavily affected the enrollment figures.

We entered the main doors. Teresa and I signed in and introduced our friends, "married couple" Jess and Ryan. The alumnae coordinator was not available, so after meeting the principal, the secretary accompanied us around the building. Teresa had not been inside Keough since attending high school there. As we walked down the hall leading to the chapel and Joseph Maskell's office, she leaned against me. I grabbed her hand, concerned she was going to fall over. Approaching the chapel, I told the nice lady that we wanted to step inside for a moment to say a prayer. Ryan's phone was almost dead, as was mine. We never thought we would get in here and did not anticipate actually being able to take pictures or record Teresa's words. Jess ran interference, asking questions of our guide about the lockers, the kids, and the water fountain.

Meanwhile, inside the chapel, this is what transpired:

Teresa: "It's bigger. Wider. The door to the outside is right there. It was between his office and the chapel. He put me on that altar. He ejaculated on me. He made me drink his semen out of the chalice."

I put my arms around Teresa. Ryan gently sighed, "Let's get out of here."

We spent the next half hour feigning interest in different parts of the building. Back at the chapel hallway, we told the secretary we would go out that door. We saw that Maskell's office was now a science storage room. A teacher lounge next to that. The bathroom in his office, where he forced girls to douche and use enemas and to sit on the toilet while he watched, was gone. But the horrific memories remain.

We then drove up Caton Avenue to where the boys' school, Cardinal Gibbons, was now vacant, holding its own secrets of abuse by clergy. Turning onto Wilkens Avenue, we headed to Our Lady of Victory Parish, where Maskell and abuser priest John Carny had both resided. Years before, on the church sidewalk, both priests had been honored with bricks inscribed with their names. A friend of the survivors had recently removed Maskell's brick. The space in the sidewalk where the brick had been was now a gaping rectangle, almost like a miniature open grave. The remover had made sure that the brick would never again be in one piece. It was rightfully destroyed after being given to a survivor. That person smashed it with resolution. Carney's brick, larger and probably costing more, was adjacent and still there. I have often thought that all the bricks in the archdiocese that honor credibly accused priests should be removed and destroyed forever.

Leaving that site, we continued to the Carriage House Apartments, where Sister Cathy and Sister Russell lived. Hearing about the area is not the same as visiting the area. Spotlighted in a movie, it becomes a place cloaked in emotion, but it is only a normal and unremarkable neighborhood, but one where single women would likely not reside anymore. That neighborhood has changed. However, it changed for most of us the day Cathy disappeared.

Moving on, we did for the first time, drive to Monumental Avenue, where Sister Cathy's body was found. Again, a benign quiet neighborhood, which we would come to know intimately and explore during our mission to find answers. At the time of that visit, we had no idea where exactly those events happened, but it was stunning that day for me to realize that it was within walking distance of my own home. There are no coincidences.

Thus began a monthly routine with Tripod Media of meetings, filming, interviews, door-knocking and many, many rabbit holes. The next three years were a sometimes-chaotic blur of the filmmakers following me and Abbie Schaub as we continued our journey, now with microphones in our clothing and cameras in our faces. Our primary cameraman was Academy Award-winning photographer John Benam. Although credit goes to two other cameramen, Gabriel and John #2, Benam became our local contact and friend.

John and his family are one of my adopted families. I love them and their children. John and his wife Angela remain trusted confidantes. They have weathered many mishaps and disappointments with me. John's formal title is the Director of Photography for *The Keepers*. He and Jess and Ryan sometimes all had cameras aimed at us. If the filmmakers were not available to be with Abbie and me or any of the others when we were interviewing key individuals or visiting an area, John would cover us on film. If we could wait for our LA friends, we would schedule those interactions during their visits.

Our filmmakers already had a remarkable list of fine documentaries: *Good Ole' Freda*, *The Case Against Eight*, *Serena* and, more recently, *Ask Doctor Ruth*. But from what we could figure, and we did try, they were financing this project on their own. In the middle of the filming, they were invited to the Sundance Conference, in which filmmakers are invited to share their projects and be critiqued by their peers. (This is not to be confused with the Sundance Film Festival, which they have also attended.) Ryan told us that the participants were so impressed with *The Keepers* mini presentation that he and Jess were asked for more meetings than any other filmmakers there that weekend. He shared with us that investors were writing personal checks to make sure the project would be completed. None of us involved with *The Keepers* were paid for our participation, so let's put that lingering rumor to rest. We did each sign a release form, agreeing that anything we said or did on film could be used in the series. I never have figured out how in the world suspect Edgar Davidson was coaxed into signing that form. But he did. Perhaps in some corner of his aging mind, he was prepared to say more about what he knew. We know he knew Cathy because he called her "Cathy," not Sister Catherine, and we think Davidson knew Maskell because he did not identify him as "Father." He simply called him "Maskell." But Edgar's secrets also went to the grave with him when he died in 2018. I do not know what the police know about Davidson, but some of us think that maybe there is telltale DNA on some of those weird stuffed toys who lived in their own bedroom of an apartment he shared with his third wife.

I never knew what to expect when Ryan and Jessica came to

town. It could be knocking on doors, filming my phone calls, or doing pick-up lines. Pick-up lines are not recorded so that I could get picked up by strange guys in bars, which I know you all are thinking. Pick-ups, I learned, are a bunch of follow-up questions they would ask me based on the footage of me they had reviewed. It would go something like this: "What impact did Cathy have on you?" "How would you describe her teaching?" "What is Abbie's best investigative skill?" There might be several unrelated questions asked one after the other and my responses were inserted into the audio or video where needed to fill in some blanks. You saw all that. What you did not see was me falling down in cemeteries, on ice, and in the snow trying to read VIN numbers on old junky cars. Once, while wearing a mike, I used the F word as I tripped on a wooded hillside and landed with a branch between my legs. Got the picture? Ouch.

During the making of *The Keepers*, we often ate meals together. Usually at the Double T Diner at Route 40 West and Rolling Road in Catonsville, Maryland. The waitress soon knew us and always put us in the same corner so as not to disturb others or be disturbed if the cameras came out. The evenings when filming was at my house gave me the opportunity to entertain my guests. Because I do not cook, I usually impressed everyone with what I called charcuterie—basically cheese, crackers, pepperoni, and Fritos. When I have guests, my treat is to buy a dozen small gourmet ice creams and pass the plastic store bag of them around. Even the cups have their own wooden spoons. You saw one of my attempts at cooking real food in the series, so we do not need to go there, okay?

One of the most memorable events for me during filming was certainly the day we met retired police lieutenant James Scannell. His family has denied emphatically his role in any abuse and possibly in Cathy's death, but my opinion is that he did not tell us the truth. His responses to questions that were not shared in *The Keepers* included remarks that the Keough girls told stories of abuse because teenagers like attention. But the survivors' stories were the same. The girls did not know that their classmates were telling the same stories. Women who recognized Scannell in *The Keepers* alleged that he was one of their abusers, a friend of Edgar and buddies with Maskell. And yes, I'm going to tell you my theory of what happened to Cathy and what happened to Joyce. Hang on. Be patient. It's coming.

My experience meeting Cathy's family, especially her sister Marilyn, changed my life. What you saw in the docuseries was filmed as it was happening. You missed me falling over a table in the hotel lobby, but everything else was authentic. Marilyn Cesnik Radakovic is one of the most gracious, sweet and kind women I have ever met. Yes, very much like Cathy. We connected immediately. We get each other. We laugh at the same things. We cry without apology. My hours with her and her husband, Bob, are precious to me. Until Ann Cesnik (Cathy and Marilyn's mother) died, the rest of the family knew nothing about Maskell, abuse, or the suspicions of who killed Cathy. It took months before Marilyn was comfortable talking to me. I thank her daughter, Cathy, for facilitating that. Cathy Joanita is named for her aunt, Sister Cathy. I had the unique opportunity to meet the whole family in the summer of 2017; I will never forget being with them and feeling like part of their family.

My own family knew nothing about my involvement in finding out who hurt Cathy and the surrounding stories of abuse. My mom, then ninety-one, would worry, and my siblings would not get me at all. When my mom was diagnosed with colon cancer, our family life centered around spending time with her. *The Keepers* was a distraction that kept me from totally losing myself in grief and sadness. Some days, I would return home from her apartment, and my filmmaker friends would be there waiting for me with open arms and food. Food from my own refrigerator. Ryan had a crush on Fresca—yes, the soda. In my family, we call that drink "Flicka" because, as a toddler, my niece, Charlotte, could not say "Fresca." If Ryan was headed to Baltimore, there was always a case of Flicka in my refrigerator. One time, when he asked if I had any Flicka, I laughed out loud. He got a case of it for his birthday.

When I finally shared the project with my sister Maria, who had also attended Keough, and introduced her to Tripod, she calmly said, "Gem, this is your tribe now." You saw the art studio my sister and her husband George operate in the first episode, because it is directly next to The Caton Tavern, scene of many Yellow Tail jokes and my go-to line "I'm not hitting on you, but do you have any baggage?" The Staub Art Studio, named for my mom, Cecilia Staub, has a long and honorable legacy in the Catonsville area. My mother's death in 2015 sent all our lives and plans in different directions.

The release of *The Keepers* in May 2017 ushered in a whirlwind of attention, interviews, news articles. Having to buy TV clothes was so weird for me. I was assigned a Netflix person to schedule my interviews. Judgments and opinions about what we had done were written, spoken, and displayed for the world to view. Living alone with my dog, Teddy, became living on a stage. Messages from all over the world arrived daily. I got sick. For weeks. A respiratory illness and ear infection prevented me from walking straight. And I could barely drag my dog outside without someone recognizing me practically stumbling down the street. I resorted to sunglasses and a big hat.

The release of the Netflix series in May 2017 was unprecedented. My life was changed forever. "How did I get here?" I said repeatedly that summer. Now I think I have those answers.

PART TWO

The Way I Was

3

Little Gemma

"Hi. This is Gemma Hoskins. You may know me from *The Keepers*." This is how I start every conversation when I call a radio or TV station, an attorney, abuse hotline, politician, cop, celebrity, or anybody that I ask for help or offer to help.

I used to hate my name. When I was a kid, nobody knew how to spell it or pronounce it. On Valentine's Day in second grade, all I remember is looking through tears with an achy throat at the envelopes on my desk. Jema, Gemini, Gema, Gina. Some kids even decorated around the misspelled letters. Only my best friend, Mary Jo, spelled it right. And that was because our moms were also friends. Mary Jo and I practiced writing our names for a year before we started school. I do not have a middle name. And to me, she did not either. I always call Mary Jo her whole name, not Mary. I never thought of Jo as a middle name. As a young adult, however, I began to kind of dig my name. I could use just my first name and people knew it was me. It was like Cher, Madonna, and me, Gemma. Today, my name opens doors. It gets me through to the hosts on radio shows.

Celebrities friend me on Facebook; some even follow me on Twitter. My most famous friend right now is Chris Hanson, the guy that catches the sexual predators. Every day, somebody says, "Are you Gemma?" Recently, a lady stopped me while I was walking Teddy on the street and said, "Is that the dog from *The Keepers*?" I eyed her over my sunglasses. "Uh, yeah."

I can remember back to when I was two. Vividly. No misty-colored memories for me of the way I was. I used to ask my mom when certain things I remembered happened, so I know my memories are accurate and confirmed. A fire in the neighborhood. Dad's car rolling down the street with nobody in it and seeing it smash into the back of another car down the street. My sister running away from me at the playground. Winning a "Best Baby Doll Award" at the same playground. And then there was Mr. Brown next door, hauling all the kids on the block into the back of his red pickup truck, then Mom running out yelling, "Stop that, George! You take that child out of that truck!" I remember him lifting me in and mom lifting me out. Everybody else got to go for the two-minute ride around our very short block. I was crying for being left out. I cried a lot in my life for being left out. But that's for later.

I was a smart kid at two. I could—and still can—name all the people in order on the block and what they looked like. The Cleavengers were first. Mrs. Cleavenger grew strawberries in her back yard and put them on our back porch in little green cardboard boxes. I would see her picking them and then peek to see if she had left the treasure for us. Funny, I never saw her actually lean over the metal fence and put them there, but they always appeared right before dinner. They were probably the best strawberries I ever ate. Next on the block was us, the Staubs. I have my house inside and out memorized—not from photos, but from those little movie screens we keep private on the inside of our eyelids. Doesn't everybody have those?

My dad painted our front concrete porch bright red. Thick, shiny semi-gloss. I would love to have a red porch now, but back then we thought it was normal. (Wouldn't my HOA have a field day dealing with a Gemma-red porch now?) We had a black-and-white TV in the living room. I can see it in the corner of the room, with its bulging screen that was square with rounded corners. Mom once mail-ordered a piece of transparent film that came with fat colored crayons from the Mickey Mouse Club, and when Mickey came on, he would tell us to get our magic screen and stick it on the front of the TV. It stuck by static electricity. The Mousketeer in charge, Jimmy Somebody, would draw on his easel. I traced his lines on my magic screen, and Dumbo or Donald would appear in front of my wondering eyes. I was an artist! I think that was such a cool idea way back then in 1954.

There was a blue rocking chair in that front room as well. I remember sitting in it, rocking ferociously with my GEMMA bracelet on—one of those bracelets, where each tiny bead was a letter of my name. (In those days, things like that did not break. Nowadays, the same bracelet would not be the same bracelet. Now I think they break as soon as you put the cheap rubber cord around your wrist.) The blue chair had a music box on the rocker part so that when I rocked, a song would play. I have known Brahms Lullaby all my life, so I have a feeling it was that one. I sing "Lullaby and Good Night" to Teddy even now.

My bedroom was in the back, and I shared it with my sister, Toni, and our baby sister, Maria. It looked out on the backyard where we had a glider that we could sit on and hit the fences on each side when we pushed. I remember so much about this house and neighborhood, and I want to tell you everything because it was such a happy time for me. I want to cram it all in whether it fits or not.

Next on the block were the Browns. Tommy and Bobby. Their dad was the red pickup truck man. I met up with those guys in college, but their names are so common, I never tried to find them on Facebook. Maybe now they will try to find me. Next to the Browns were the Morrisetts: Izetta and Clifford, and their kids, Francis Lee and Little Clifford. Little Clifford was about seven feet tall, but he was still called Little. Izetta let me help her pack boxes when they were moving. She had all that Home Accents stuff, like candle sconces and filigree wall hangings. I thought they were beautiful treasures. Wrapping them in newspaper with care and placing each into boxes was such a treat. But Little Clifford had a pet squirrel. In the house. He let it out of the cage. It ran up my arm and onto my head. I froze. Then screamed. That's all I remember. Talk about repressed memories.

There was a big fire one night in the Morrissett's house. Somebody left a cigarette burning in the basement, and it ignited a couch. Izetta is dead now, so I guess it's okay to say I think she was the culprit. In the middle of the night, the street was filled with fire trucks, sirens, yelling and screaming. There was Izetta, lying on the front lawn in her nightgown with her robe open. My dad ran out and covered her up. I don't think he checked to see if she was alive—he just covered her up. My mom let us look out the back-bedroom window to keep us from looking at Izetta, I guess. The Morrissett's laundry was hung out on their clothesline. All of it was covered in soot. Black and gray and stiff, like invisible bodies were inside. I could draw that creepy image for you, it is so indelible.

Next and last on the block were the Lundbergs. Christine was the same age as my older sister, Toni. After *The Keepers* came out, a woman named Christine got in touch and told me she was Christine Lundberg. I told her I had written a poem about her, about the time she came to see us in our new house. Christine Lundberg, I hope you are reading this. I did not want to offend you by sending it to you, but here is that poem, and you can read it if you want to. It's not all that nice about you. Otherwise, you can skip this part.

Christine Lundberg Came To Visit

Christine Lundberg came to visit us
in the new house.
She lived on the corner of the block
at our old house.
A cloudy spring day, I can see it clearly
In our backyard
On our sidewalk
Near our playground.
She wore a dress
(I think Mrs. Lundberg made her wear something nice).
I lived there so I had on a skort with Keds.
She couldn't get dirty on the playground out back
even though I could tell from her face
She was dying to do that.
The gray day made me sad,
There was nothing to do.
I forgot the excitement of Christine coming
and wished she would just go home
So we could have our Sunday Lipton chicken noodle soup-and-
*   sandwich supper*
Alone.

Did you ever play "Would you rather?" I did. Two of us would name our favorite color or car or toy or shoes and then we would say to the third friend, "Would you rather have blue or red?" "Sky-blue or grape popsicles?" (Of course, sky-blue always won because it was a special flavor that the Good Humor man did not always have.) Or "Hamburgers or hot dogs?" When the third friend picked one, they would get to take the place of the person who came up with it to begin with. Hardly ever did anybody ever pick the selection I offered. As far back as those days, I felt like something was different about me. Maybe everybody felt that way. I only know I was looking out of my head with my little eyes, thinking everybody else had something I did not have, or that I had something they did not. But mostly I thought the first.

I had a mostly fun childhood, but shit hit the fan early for me. I had chicken pox on the Christmas after my third birthday. That was the year I got a big metal dollhouse that had sharp edges and plastic furniture small enough to choke on. I did not get cut or choke. Nothing poked my eye out. But I had to lie on the couch with my pox itching and reach over to the floor to move all the little stuff around in that dangerous toy. I think I was upchucking too and had to aim away from the dollhouse to the bucket on the floor.

There always seemed to be some other unfair health issue following me around. A virus hospitalized me at the age of four. I remember being in a pale-blue ward full of kids in Baltimore's famous Bons Secours Hospital. I was also born there. I liked to say "Bahn Suckore," having no idea what it meant. Or that is was French. The ward I was in probably had five or six sets of beds, each pair divided by a piece of glass. Facing the room, I was on the right side of the glass. I could peek over and see a boy on the other side looking back at me. There was ick on the glass, I guess from us peeking and sniffling and sticking our tongues out at each other. He could move around more than I could because I had intravenous needles in the front of my thighs. I thought they were some sort of clothespins with hoses attached. I must have been very sick. I was in that bed with those needles for days. I did sort of wonder if the glass was ever cleaned. Maybe after I was gone and before another child was admitted.

Back then, parents could only visit for a short time during the day. My younger sister, Maria, had just been born, and my older sister was in kindergarten. I think our neighbor had a daughter who was a small person, back then called a dwarf. She came over and babysat while my mom tried to see me. I bet Mom rode a bus or took a cab to get there. After a while, Mom figured out that if she could send my dad in each evening with something I had supposedly "forgotten," that the hospital would let him come in and see me for a few minutes. The first time he brought me a clean pair of pajamas. The next time he brought my "Gemma" doll. Gemma was made of rubber, about six inches tall, but a baby doll. Only her head moved around. All the way around. I used to put her head on backwards and think it was so funny. Gemma had rubber hair that was bumpy and painted on. At home, I would line up my dolls on each side of my head on the pillow and lie very still in the center. Gemma was always next to my head because I chewed on her rubber hair every night. I am certain I ingested toxic chemicals eating her head. Before I went to sleep, I would call my mom to say I was ready. Mom kissed each doll in the row and then Gemma-doll and real Gemma last. She said goodnight to all of them.

I remember that there was another doll I made from a kit of two pieces of printed felt cloth. She had a large flat head like a gingerbread girl or lollipop. I had learned to sew a long piece of yarn, using a big fake needle, through holes punched around the edge of her flat body. Right near the end, I would stuff her with cotton balls. I think Grandma finished her off with stitching so nothing would fall out. Once, I got mustard on her shirt and it never came out.

So, the day I was released from Bon Secours Hospital after my virus, I sat in a wee blue rocking chair on the floor in front of a little black-and-white television. I was watching the Mickey Mouse Club. My mom came up behind me and leaned all the way over my head. I looked at her upside-down face. She said "Hi, Gem. You ready to come home?" I reached my arms up and held the sides of her beautiful face like I could never let her go away again. This is still one of my sweetest memories of my mother.

Ear abscesses and tonsillitis followed soon after. But this is not a total tale of woe. I had nothing to compare this to, so I guess I did not complain much, except when the earaches got bad. My mom took me to the doctor who had delivered me, Dr. Thomas in Irvington, in west Baltimore. He told her to give me aspirin and put me to bed. She was a smart lady and decided to see another doctor. Doctor Frey at Edmondson Village took one look at my ears and told my mom I had abscesses that needed to be lanced. On the ear-lancing day, we went in a taxi to the Medical Arts building on Read Street in Baltimore. I was not allowed to eat. Strangely, I have since learned that this is the same office building where Dr. Christian Richter allegedly performed illegal gynecological surgeries on some of the girls Joseph Maskell raped.

I can still smell that building and would recognize it in an instant. Big mahogany bannisters and dark walls. A lady sitting in a room with what looked to me like about a dozen Q-Tips stuck up her nose with the ends hanging out like spikes. (If anybody knows what that was all about, please get in touch with me.) She did not look pleased. I climbed up on a long flat paper-covered table and a nurse put a rubber mask over my face that made me nauseous. She said it was sleeping gas. I thought it was barbaric.

When I woke up, my ears were screaming. My mom put me in another cab, and I threw up on the red cracked-vinyl seat all the way home. The cab driver stopped so Mom could go in a store and get a box of Kleenex. I remember him holding a handkerchief over his nose and saying, "There now. There now," while she was in the store. I feel like crying right now when I think of all the things my mom did for me; I loved her so much. I wanted to be her big girl. I tried not to cry, but I wept into my pillow that night due to my ear pain. Mom finally came in and gave me a capful of something called Turpin Hydrate and Codeine, which was magic. It is now considered a highly addictive narcotic, but Mom knew her shit.

By this time, my family had moved to the West Hills neighborhood on the city-county line where I would spend the rest of my childhood years. The day we moved, my parents got the house ready and brought me in. Grandma was there with Maria; Toni was at school now in the second grade at St. Bernardine's. I stepped through the front door and over a rolled-up gray rug and sat right there on that rug. Mom was eight months pregnant, and she told me later that they had forty dollars left in the bank that day. My new best friend lived a few houses away, Mary Jo Smith. Her mom went to school with my mom at Seton High School. We were both good four year olds, although Mary Jo had already turned five. Our moms took turns watching us because Mrs. Smith had a little boy Maria's age named David, and Mom was ready to pop with Jimmy. (In *The Keepers*, you see David and his wife Mary at the JRC Jewelry store they own on the day we brought the necklace Edgar Davidson gave his wife to be evaluated by their gemologist. At that time, we thought Davidson may have taken the necklace from Sister Cathy's car.)

That first year at home with my mother was heaven. There was no kindergarten at St. William of York parish school, so I was Mom's helper. I put Maria in her crib, turned on the little blue-metal record player with the yellow forty-fives and looked at her through the crib bars. She looked back. I sang all the Mickey Mouse Club days-of-the-week songs to lull her to sleep. But she never fell asleep. Maria would figure out how to get out of that crib, and I would put her back in. I can still sing every one of those songs. "Today is Tuesday, you know what that means. We're gonna have a special guest." Friday was always Talent Round-Up Day: "Saddle you ponies, here we go, down to the talent rodeo." If anybody can get me that yellow forty-five, I will gladly buy it from you.

Maria was a bumper. She would sit and bump back and forth on the crib rails, chanting, "I love Mommy. I love Daddy. I love Grandma." I always loved it when she got to my name. "I love Gemma." Meanwhile, baby-boy Jim would be in his stroller and Mom would push him back and forth gently while doing other things. Sometimes Mom would let me play in the living room while she took a nap in the nubby green chair. The chair had a loose cushion and Mom would pull her feet up in the chair and "take forty winks." That's a nap. She was an artist, so she gave me a big drawing board. She also gave me a bunch of food cans from the kitchen cabinet. I peeled all the labels off the cans and made towers and towns during the forty winks she was taking. We never knew what we were having for dinner in the way of canned goods because there were no labels left on them. My mom was so cool like that.

The first day of school, just before I turned six, was the most exciting thing I had ever experienced—even better than my brother being born, which I did not understand anyway. I just remember Grandma being there one morning when I woke up saying, "Your mom and dad went to get your new brother from the hospital." *Okay*, I thought. *Whatever*. The day he came home, I thought it was funny that Mom had to come in through the back door, where there were no steps for her to climb. And why was Daddy carrying her baby? A few years later, I figured out it was his baby too.

The first morning of first grade, my mom and I walked up the block to Mary Jo's house. Her mom knew how to drive, so Mary Jo and I got in the back seat. We wore our white blouses and blue jumpers, heavy dark blue sleeveless dresses, which comprised our uniforms. These dresses were adorned with something I learned was called an emblem. It was a diamond shape with SWS inside for Saint William's School. The jumpers were new only to us. Some other SWS girls had outgrown them, so our moms bought them used at the school. However, we did each have new saddle shoes and white socks. The ride to school was short, but I was sure I was going to wet my pants.

Our classroom was on the first floor of the school looking out on the asphalt playground. We sat on little chairs in the hallway waiting for our names to be called. Our moms sat on the little chairs with us. *Smith* and *Staub* were always called near the end. When we got called, we both ended up in Sister Marian Joseph's class. Forty-eight of us sitting in six rows of eight desks. I loved Sister. She was tall and thin and so pretty. We read books about Dick and Jane and their white family: Dad worked, Mom stayed home cleaning in a dress and nice heels. One dog, Spot. One cat, Zip. In the story, when the black family moved into the neighborhood, we had questions for Sister. I think she said we would skip that story. I recently paid twenty bucks in an antique store for one of those darn Dick and Jane books because I wanted to read the story about the black family. The word "diversity" had not yet been invented.

Mary Jo and I were both in the Bluebirds group. Bluebirds were the top kids. I have no clue what the other groups were; I was just excited to be a Bluebird. When Sister called out Bluebirds, a bunch of us dragged our little chairs to the front of the room. Other kids who were not Bluebirds would stick their feet out to trip us. Sister had a huge copy of the same reading story book we had (now they are called Big Books). She sat with us in a semicircle and turned the pages of her book like Vanna White. With grace and panache. And without ever taking an eye off the rest of the class behind us. We went around the circle taking turns reading the pages. Sometimes, I guess if her arm was tired, she would let one of us turn the pages of her big book. But kids picked on you if you were the page-turner. They called you the teacher's pet. I hated being the page-turner, but I got that job a lot. Being the teacher's pet is an awful label to have. It meant getting punished by other kids for being smart. Now it's called bullying, and it is against the law.

I also got the job of collecting the fat red pencils from all the kids and sharpening them. The pencils were a dark ruby color with chew marks from all our crooked teeth. The kids would stick them in a box lid Sister had created with forty-eight holes in it for holding the pencils, just like the room: six rows of eight. I was number forty-one, which put me in the last row by the window. The box lid made sure the kids would get their own chewed-up pencil back. Just shorter and sharper. If the kids had not gotten their original pencil back, I am sure they would have ended up with pencil PTSD.

Growing up in a Catholic family is the only thing I know, so I have nothing with which to compare it. The kids who did not go to St. William's school when I did were thought of as "publics." To me, there were Catholics and Publics. Publics wore regular clothes to school, not uniforms. They seemed way more worldly to me and, actually, I was kind of afraid of them, like maybe they were teenagers when they were eleven. Hairspray and lipstick. Sweaters that fit. Short skirts and stockings. Yeah, *worldly*.

I was taught mostly by nuns for twelve years. The nuns at St. Will's were the School Sisters of the Union of the Sacred Heart. I can't figure out why, but their label was SUSC. I do not know what the C stands for, but the sisters told us to remember to "Send Us Some Candy," which I thought was funny. My mom told us they could not keep any presents we gave them: they had to share gifts with the other sisters. They lived in a convent attached to the school. A convent is like a hotel for nuns but without separate bathrooms or air conditioning. My cousin was a nun at St. Will's—Sister Margaret Kernan. My mom got to see her room once and said it was plain with only a twin bed and crucifix on the wall above the bed. Jesus was hanging on that cross, watching Sister Margaret sleep. I have never been in a prison cell but have seen plenty on television, and I have a feeling cells are very much like the convent rooms but with bars. But even a cell has a sink and a toilet.

When I was around ten, I got to go inside the convent to help a couple nuns carry some posters for the parish carnival to the school hall. I went down into the basement with some other girls to get the goods. At the bottom of the steps to the basement were clotheslines, and on them was underwear. Bras and underpants and long white slips, all hanging in the basement. I could not stop looking. I remember wondering who the fattest sisters were because some of their undergarments were huge. I don't think they bought this stuff at the Hecht's or Hochschild's where my mom bought hers. I guess the sisters did not want anybody walking or driving by the school on Edmondson Avenue to see all their intimate garments blowing in the breeze. The sister waiting for us to get the posters yelled down the steps to hurry up and stop being nosy.

At Christmastime, Mom saved the boxes in which religious Christmas cards were purchased. When we made cookies, we lined those boxes with aluminum foil and packed the boxes as presents of cookies for the SUSC nuns. Because I knew they had to share, I always liked when my teacher would open it and take a few Tollhouse cookies out at lunchtime for herself. She figured out how to get around that sharing rule.

On the first Friday of each month, we went to Mass before school. Dad would drop us off in front of the church on his way to work. After Mass, we got to go into the classroom late if the priest gave a really long sermon. But on those days, we also got to eat a packed breakfast in the classroom. If you went to Communion, you could not eat for a couple hours before church. Having my packed breakfast with a six-cent glass bottle of milk while reading my Weekly Reader or my library book made Fridays bearable.

I received my First Confession and First Communion in second grade. Confession was terrifying. The whole class went over to the church one day and sat in the pews waiting until it was time for our row to line up. My knees were knocking together. I had a piece of net called a chapel veil on my head, stuck in place with a bobby pin. Girls had to cover their heads in church. Some of the older girls wore something called a mantilla, which looked like long hair, made from the same chapel veil netting. On Sundays, hats were allowed but not on schooldays.

The confessional was a brown wooden box that looked like an outhouse. There was a curtain on one side to go behind, and inside was a kneeler in front of a window. When the priest heard you come in and kneel, he slid the partition in the window back. The priest sat sideways and usually put his head on his hand and his elbow on the ledge of the window. I always hoped he was listening, but I think a lot of the time he was sleeping. "Bless me Father for I have sinned. This is my first confession, and these are my sins." Sins . . . at seven years old. "I was disrespectful to my parents three times (or was it four times?). I told a lie to my grandmother when she asked me if I wanted milk or soda pop, and I said milk." After telling my sins, the priest would tell me to say three Hail Marys and three Our Fathers and an Act of Contrition. The Act of Contrition was a "sorry" prayer. I think you had to say it while you were still on the kneeler. "Oh my God, I am heartily sorry for having offended thee, and I detest all my sins." I've said that prayer a hundred times, but I forget the rest of it. My sister Maria told me once that if she said the wrong number of times for a sin, she would get back in line and tell the priest she lied about that number.

Now, this confession thing created a ton of guilt and fear and confusion—for me and a lot of kids. Fortunately, nothing bad ever happened to me inside that box, but I was so afraid of the priest that, as I grew older, I avoided confession completely. I guess that means I did not receive Communion in a state of grace. But it also means I did not have the unfortunate experience of dealing with pedophile priests at Keough, stalking their prey in the confessional. I never once went to confession in the Keough chapel. I don't even know why. At St. William's, each confessional started posting a little name tag to say which priest was inside. And if the priest forgot to change the name tag, a parishioner would have a big surprise. Father Kinsella was nice and talked to us like real people. Father Albert, the pastor, was authoritarian and stern. Father Brannan, I think, had a few sips of altar wine back there to get through all the sinners.

First Communion was a huge part of second grade. I guess we did a lot of getting ready. Because I was very tall and my last name was

Staub, I was always near the end of the line for everything. (That's also why I did not attend my college graduation from Towson University. Going to Ocean City was much more appealing than waiting two hours for my name to be called to walk across a stage and get my diploma from a stranger. My whole family had better things to do.) So, I was at the end of the line of girls waiting to go up to the altar for communion. My side-by-side partner was Gail Wires. (I wonder how Gail is doing these days.) Knees knocking again, we proceeded to the long marble altar rail and knelt. The priest came along with a chalice full of little white disks called *hosts*. An altar boy who was not in the communion class would walk along with the priest and hold a metal dish called a *paten* under your chin, in case the host fell off your tongue. The boy always looked like he wanted to burst out laughing looking at our pious faces. I was never sure what to do when we returned to our seats. I knelt and closed my eyes tightly and tried not to gag as I tried to unstick the dry wafer from the top of my mouth. It was a lot of work.

The rest of First Communion day was like Easter. Everybody dressed up, me in my mini white wedding dress (weird), and ate a big Sunday dinner. I remember getting a prayer book with my name in gold on the plastic cover, as well as a little crucifix to wear around my neck and a bigger one to hang on the wall above my bed so Jesus could watch me sleeping too.

After that, I thought going to Mass every Sunday, and on all the extra required days, was boring. My dad would go to Mass early on Sundays for something called the Holy Name Mass and Communion Breakfast. That left Mom to get the rest of us ready and out the door for nine o'clock Mass. We walked across the street and around to the alley behind the Johnson's house. We stood at the entrance to their yard, which was really a parking pad, while Mrs. Johnson backed out the station wagon. (In the front of the Johnson's house was the public bus stop, so there was no room for their car on the street.) And off we would all go to church. If one of us said we were sick to get out of going to church, my mom would say that was fine, but if we were too sick for Mass, we were too sick to play outside. We usually got better fast enough to get ready for Mass.

Sunday clothing is a huge deal for Catholic kids. Every year, a new hat called a birdcage was worn, or a straw hat with a ribbon. A birdcage was a little Jackie Kennedy pillbox number, with a net that covered one's eyes. Strange and incredibly irritating. I preferred straw hats, which I still wear on the beach. Sunday coats—and later stockings, girdles and gloves—were part of our ensemble. Girdles at thirteen . . . go figure.

Most of the time in school I was minimally afraid of the nuns, just enough to behave—which I would have done most of the time anyway. If I had to ask my nun-teacher something, I felt like I was going to pee or cry or both. In eighth grade, when I got my first period, I went to school feeling like my uterus was going to fall on the floor. In those days, we wore a pad with an elastic waist strap with hooks to hold the pad. Asking to use the "lavatory" (there are no "bathrooms" at Catholic school) more than once that day, outside of a time when the whole class went, was a nightmare. I think the nun took mercy on me and said yes because of the painful look on my face. It never occurred to me that they were going through the same thing. However, they did have those long black dresses on.

The nuns did not mess around, even the nice ones. The priests were another story. They walked around the school and playground like they owned the place, because I guess they did. There were usually two or three priests that lived in the rectory house across from the church on the corner of Cooks Lane and Edmondson

Avenue. During the making of *The Keepers*, I learned that St. William's was the same parish Jean and Mike Wehner attended Mass with their kids.

Father Brannan was the first priest I recall. He always had a red face and looked like he was going to have a heart attack at any minute. He liked the altar wine, I think. Father John Albert was the pastor next. He was a grandfatherly type. He wore a French beret and helped the custodian, Louie, shovel the snow off the parking lot. At report-card time, Father Albert came into each classroom, sat down at the teacher's desk, and called each kid to come up and look at the report card with him. I hated those days. I got all As and Father Albert would make a huge deal over me. I was tortured the rest of the day by kids calling me teacher's pet and goody-two-shoes. When I returned later as an adult in my forties for a parish reunion, one of those boys asked me what I was doing. When I said I was a teacher, he answered, just as if we were still children, "Yeah, you always were a goody-two-shoes." In my skinny black dress with ample cleavage and black stilettos, I smiled and replied, "And you always were an asshole." I blew him a kiss, flipped him the bird, and pranced off. Nobody puts Gemma in the corner anymore.

In second grade, I fell in love with Kevin Foley. I loved him for a long time. Our teacher was Sister Barbara Thomas, who put me next to Kevin to help him. Kevin had failed first grade. How does someone fail first grade? He was funny and put apples on his head and stuck his whole face in the water fountain. His nickname was Kedgy. His brother, who did not fail first grade, had to be in another class so they would not fool around together. Later, in eighth grade, when I was still in love with Kevin, he stuck a pencil in my ear while we were practicing for our high school entrance exams. I was sure he loved me back.

When third grade rolled around, I got braces on my teeth. My teeth were a mess. Everybody else in the family had nice teeth. Not me. I had tiny teeth like Grandma had; I also had too many. When my second teeth came in, some had to be extracted before the braces could be attached. My mom would wait until the night before an extraction to tell me that I did not have to go to school the next day. But the next words out of her mouth were that I was going to the dentist. Over and over for weeks. In my mind, the dentist came at me with pliers and a wicked smile on his face. Molars came out, roots and all. (I kept one. I still have it in a tiny pink gift box, with a lock of my third-grade hair.) Sore gaping holes. Afternoons on the couch with wet tea bags on my gums, waiting for Mary Jo to bring me my homework.

The day I got the braces, Mom and I rode the bus to the orthodontist in Westview Park. Dr. Edward Kelly decked me out in metal with more metal. He used a tool to tighten the braces on each tooth, tighter and tighter. For a treat, my mom took me to the lunch counter at G.C. Murphy's in Westview Mall. I asked for my favorite going-out lunch: tuna salad on toast with chips and a 7-Up. Opening wide, I crunched into the sandwich and stopped mid-bite. My mouth ached so bad I could not eat the rough toast, and the chips cut my gums. Tears welled up. My mom was spending this money on me, and I could not even eat. How was I going to live like this for the next five years? I ate soup for days. And milkshakes, but no more gum or toast or chips for me.

One afternoon after getting my braces, I broke a Mom-rule and tried to walk up the sliding board on the West Hills playground. Holding on to the metal sides, in my bare feet (also breaking a Mom-rule), I made my way to the top, edging up the slide. Just as I reached the top, my sweaty little hands slipped, and I smacked my face directly on the slide. My railroad tracks cut the insides of my mouth, slamming my face with excruciating pain. I heard three friends screaming, "Help! Help! Gemma is bleeding to death!" The biggest of the three walked up the slide too and turned me around. We slid down together, she endlessly uttering, "Ew. Ew. Ew." One friend ran ahead to tell my mom I was dying. The other two took me by the arms and told me to close my eyes and not look. With closed eyes and dripping chin, they carefully guided me to the back door of my house. I looked. Looking back at me was a reflection in the glass door of Hannibal Lecter after having friends for lunch. I spent the rest of the day on the couch, alternating bloody ice packs with bloody popsicles. From then on, every morning my mom would melt paraffin wax in a tiny cook pot that I called my "braces pot." With her fingers, she covered my braces with lumps of the smooth wax. By the end of the school day, dry hunks of wax were falling out onto my desk. I was miserable. But I never complained. I did what I was asked and tried hard not to cry. But when I lay in my bed at night, with just one doll, I asked Jesus, Mary, and Joseph to come down to earth and let me see them. I wanted them to see what was in my mouth. They never showed up. All I could see were the silhouettes of the plastic horses I collected on the shelves up high. I could see out my window into the black night. The traffic light on the highway blinked red then green; I counted the seconds till the next color. I could hear the air brakes of the buses on the corner of the block, stopping for nobody. Out there, somewhere, something was waiting for me. I wasn't supposed to know about it yet. But what was it? And why?

Nancy Drew and the Lamppost

Sitting on the grass under the light on the corner
Oblivious to gnats and moths and lightning bugs for once
Mary Jo and I read our Nancy Drew books at night
In the summer
Well, maybe it wasn't night
Maybe it was evening
But it was getting dark
Well, maybe not dark, but sort of dim
But many pages turned, at least one
every time our brothers rode their bikes around the block
and passed us in our little light tent.

4

60 Pounds of Vulnerability

In the fall of 1962, just before my tenth birthday, I started losing weight. Already too skinny, I was always hungry, always thirsty. My mom had a cousin who had diabetes and was familiar with the symptoms. I was peeing constantly and embarrassed to tell Mom that I was itchy down there. I was in the fifth grade, so being an itchy girl who peed too much and needed more than my ten seconds at the water fountain was problematic. The kid whose responsibility it was to hold the fountain handle and count to ten always told me to hurry up, that I was drinking more than my share of whatever water was in the fountain. Unless it was Mary Jo. She would count very slowly for me.

Dr. Frey told my mom that I needed a blood test and a urine specimen. He sent us across his office waiting room to a different physician, Dr. Clifford Ratliff. Of course, my urine was full of sugar, hence the itching. I screamed the whole time Ratliff's nurse was taking my blood. Taking blood was torture in those days, not an art like it is now. I remember her no-nonsense pale face and red hair pulled back in a French twist. Mom tried to distract me, but I was no dummy. I yelled my throat dry until the nurse was finished poking the inside of my bony elbow. I think she liked hurting me. If she is still alive, she is going to know I am talking about her. Too bad, mean lady in white.

Being diagnosed at ten years old with type 1 diabetes was a novelty for me because I had no idea what was ahead. As it turned out, it involved many more blood tests. Also peeing in a cup and dropping tablets in to see what color my urine would turn. Dark blue was good, bright orange was not good. I had a lot of bright orange specimens. I was admitted to St. Agnes Hospital for two weeks in January of 1963 to learn how to be diabetic. My nurse, Mrs. Keys, had to teach me how to give myself a needle. She came in my room the first day with an orange and a bottle of water for me to practice. I got the hang of sticking the needle in the bottle and withdrawing the solution. Jamming it into the orange was kind of fun. The orange got full and mushy with water. Then Mrs. Keys told me I had to stick her in her shoulder. I said no. She said I had to. She was brave I guess, but I just could not do it. No way. The next day, Mrs. Keys came back and showed my mom how to stick her in the arm and inject saline solution from a vial. Good job, Mom. This time, I sort of did it with my mother, who let go and I did it myself. Mrs. Keys did not pass out, yell, or die. That night, it was Daddy's turn. He did not shake. He bit his lip. His teeth were clenched. He drew up the saline, held the syringe and aimed. The solution shot out of the needle all the way across the room to where another kid was recuperating from appendix surgery. We were terrible at learning this, I thought. But by the time I got to go home, I was at least jamming that syringe into my thigh and pushing the plunger. All with my eyes closed.

My naïve acceptance of counting food exchanges and calories was more like solving math problems to me. But I hated hospital food, which was portioned out for my new diabetic diet. There was always some kind of bean on the plate: French green, cut green, yellow wax, lima, kidney. I hated them all and never ate one of them. But my plate was always empty. Nobody ever knew, until now, that I was shoving those beans into the envelopes of the get-well cards that were delivered to me from classmates and neighbor ladies. I did not die from not eating beans, so I guess it was not really that big a deal. If your kid is diabetic, don't force the beans.

I was very homesick while in St. Agnes Hospital because visiting hours were limited. When my mom went home in the afternoon to be there when my siblings got home from school, I would sit in the area by the fifth-floor elevators until my dad showed up at six o'clock. I sat looking out at the traffic on Wilkens Avenue at the people heading home in the dark to warm houses that smelled like mashed potatoes and pork chops. Never-ending traffic lights, headlights, tail lights, and flashing red police cars and ambulances sirening up to the hospital emergency entrance. I was just so lonely and sad. I missed school, my bed, my homework, and being normal. The minutes crawled by. As an adult, I feel guilty now thinking about the arrangements my parents made in order to support me throughout that hospital stay.

One Sunday afternoon, both Mom and Dad came to visit. Because the other kids were home with my sister Toni, then thirteen, they could not stay long. Sometimes Toni was not the best babysitter. She had a lot of friends in the neighborhood, and sometimes her version of babysitting was yelling in the back door from the yard to make sure nobody was dead or hurt, fighting or choking. When Mom asked me if it was okay for them to leave, I could not look at them, but nodded my head. It was that time on Sunday afternoons when the weekend is winding down and everybody is sort of mellow but thinking about getting ready for the week to come. Mom and Dad left the room. I started softly crying into my stupid stiff pillow with that hospital laundry smell. My parents must have been in the hallway outside my door, because a few minutes later, my mom came back in and took her coat off. She said Daddy would come back and get her later, because she could not think of anything she wanted to do more than be with me. We colored for the rest of the afternoon. Mom was an artist, so she would draw the pictures for us to color. She also drew paper dolls with little tabs on their shoulders on shirt cardboard so that I had something fun and special to do when she left besides shoving beans into envelopes.

Understanding now that some of my friends did not have the kind of family I had, I treasure such memories. I was loved and safe and always cared for. Nobody hurt me or scared me or touched me, except to hug or say, "I love you, Gem."

Returning to school with my new learning was interesting. I would take one shot of insulin each morning. Period. The drug was called Ultralente and was long-acting. But Dr. Ratliff did not really grasp that my blood sugar would be up and down all day and then come crashing down at night. He did the best he could, but there was not a lot known about how insulin worked with children in 1963. Low blood sugar feels awful, shaky, sweaty, unstable, scary. But I would get something sweet, like a candy bar or a Coke, so sometimes it was worth it. My teacher that year was not a nun. It was Mrs. Einstein, and she and my mom were friends. I was supposed to eat something halfway through the morning. This was going to be tricky. But again, my mom had it figured out. Every day at ten thirty, Mrs. Einstein would nod her head at me and that was my signal to go downstairs and out the front door of the school. Mom would be waiting for me with a wax paper bag of carefully measured peanut butter on eight saltine crackers. She would sit with me on the school steps while I ate my snack and drank from a little Thermos of water or iced tea. Mom acted like this was the most fun thing in the world to be doing in the middle of the morning with a four-year-old at home. But she was there every day for a few weeks until I got the hang of this new normal. Many days, if the weather was nice, we had recess around eleven o'clock. I brought my cracker sandwiches and walked around the asphalt parking lot we called the school playground eating them quickly. I was embarrassed, and the boys knew it. They would run over to the girls' side of the parking lot and steal my wax-paper bag. I panicked. Then I learned to eat faster and farther away from the invisible dividing line between the boys' side and the girls' side. Somehow I managed to learn more than my doctors did back then and was able to get through these challenges until combining insulins and counting carbohydrates became the way to manage diabetes.

Being set apart because of my health issues made me an easy target. I hated having to have a different treat or no treat. I hated having to carry Lifesavers and not wanting anybody to know I needed to eat them when my blood sugar dropped. I worried that if a substitute teacher saw me sneaking my hand under my squeaky desk lid to grab a few candies to jam into my jaws, I would get in trouble. Even going bowling after school with the other kids on a bus to the Fairlanes at Westview meant that someone's mom who drove in the neighborhood would have to bring me a bottle of Tab sugar-free soda and my cracker sandwiches. She would run into the bowling alley, find me, and stick my snack in a cubby near the bowling lane as discreetly as possible.

Birthday parties were the worst. When I was seven, my mom made me a cherry cake with cherry icing and a whole jar of maraschino cherries poured on it. Now my cake was some lame sugar-free cookies with cream cheese and pineapple in between. My mom made it in an ice-cube tray and told me it was called an icebox cake. Nah, not buying that. Going to other kids' parties with my own snacks and soda was awful too. My mom would send it all ahead, and the birthday mom would set it in front of me. Swallowing tears, I just wanted to be at home not having anything to do with a stupid party. I have a feeling my mother cried for me that I was diabetic and had to be treated differently. I know she would have traded places with me in a second. I finally gave up on cake and asked for prime rib on my birthday and got it. The end cut. With real mashed potatoes and peas. NO BEANS.

As a second-grade teacher, I promised myself that no kid would ever feel isolated because of food allergies or diabetes. If a mom was bringing in cupcakes for a kid's party, I made sure there were lots of other choices for those kids: popcorn, graham crackers with, yes, peanut butter, juice boxes and NO soda. Everybody was happy.

Turmoil in grade school in the form of bullying and being left out was a pattern that continued for me even through eighth grade. I loved school but tried to not do well and tried to get into trouble to fit in. Once my dad figured out what I was doing, that ended quickly. The day I got a "Needs Improvement" for deportment (behavior), I was so excited to show Kevin Foley. He thought it was cool. Dad did not. He went to school that evening and knocked on the convent door. He talked to Sister. Sister said I wiggled the line. Wiggled the line? I think he told her she was crazy, but he did tell me not to wiggle the line anymore.

Friendships that were not authentic broke my heart but made me stronger. My lack of worldliness and my fear of being left out made me an easy target. I was too tall, too smart, too good. My love of school and my excellence in every subject caused me so much negative attention from other kids that I misbehaved just to be punished. Being punished was kind of a status symbol. Detention with the cool kids was fun.

Not being included made me feel so bad, but I did not know why. What was I doing wrong? One school night, in eighth grade, the phone rang. A boy name Ricky asked to speak to me. Excited but confused, I got on the phone and we talked about nothing. But it was special. And fun. A few minutes after we hung up, another boy called me. This time it was Bobby. He was funny, and we laughed on the phone. This was euphoria. When the phone rang a third time, and Tim started telling me about his game, my heart sank. I could hear muffled laughter in the background. Voices. A lot of voices. I hung up heartsick and confused. The next morning, the most popular girl in the class came over to my desk and told me that all the boys from the baseball team were at her house the night before taking turns calling me. It was a cruel joke. They were pretending they liked me. I don't know how I got through the rest of the day. When I got home, I ran upstairs and stuck my head under the bathtub faucet and let the warm water run through my long hair until I stopped sobbing. When I finally emerged, my mom was in my room holding a big towel for me. I blubbered through the story. I was so humiliated and ashamed that I fell for the mean joke. I knew I could not go back to school the following Monday. Without blinking an eye, my mom looked at me and said that I could finish the year at St. Mark's school, where my cousin Eileen Nolan went. We would figure out how to go together. I thought about this all weekend. By Sunday, I decided I would stick it out at St. William's. On Monday morning, when I got to school, nobody even looked at me or said anything about what happened. They had moved on to the next vulnerable, insecure kid and I was safe for a while.

But events like this one had a serious impact on my self-esteem and confidence. I would need to learn how to deal with my doubts and fears, wondering what I was lacking. The next fifty years of my life would be a roller coaster of unexpected highs and lows. So, I learned to tough it out, to bite the bullet. That challenge remains a constant pebble in my shoe.

5

Control Freak

Living with a potentially life-threatening disease forced me to behave as an adult while still a child. Control was literally the only way I would be able to survive. Faced with no other choice, accepting that I was a diabetic was a struggle. I began a pattern of hiding my condition, privately working hard to beat it and trying relentlessly to act like everybody else. None of those behaviors were ideal or very productive. For a long time, when I met new people, I did not tell them that I had diabetes; some folks reading this will be surprised that they never knew. I was always worried about how to handle low blood sugar, which my family called "insulin reactions." In the 1960s and '70s, there were no home-monitoring devices available. I had to test how much sugar was in my urine several times a day with a little kit that looked like what is used to test the chemicals in swimming pools. Of course, reliability was always an issue, because urine sugar is rarely representative of actual blood sugar. Until home glucose monitoring arrived much later, my mom and I had only the urine sugars and monthly blood draws at Dr. Ratliff's office as guidelines.

I carried Lifesaver candies with me constantly. I grew to hate Lifesavers. At school, feeling an insulin reaction coming on meant sneaking those sticky disks into my mouth without attracting attention. In high school, the school nurse asked me to come down to her office once in my freshman year to ask if I had Lifesavers with me all the time. That was the extent of her involvement in my healthcare. This is the same woman who would later call girls to her office repeatedly to give them a pass to Reverend Joseph Maskell's office. So much for checking more than once in four years on Gemma Staub's blood sugar. Interesting that one of her jobs at Keough was also to meet with Maskell, the chaplain, Sister Judith, the dean and whoever the guidance counselor was at the time. Weekly, this group would review the names of students experiencing academic problems, family conflict or health issues. They even kept track of when everybody had their periods. Seriously. No wonder Maskell knew so much about all of us. These meetings provided him with a list of likely prey.

Independent as I was, I was still terribly concerned that I did not, at any given time, know if my blood sugar was too high or too low. I could feel shaky and sweaty if it was low, but I have a feeling that most of the school day, my glucose was high. I carried my lunch (a sandwich, fruit, and milk) every day, but like most teens, I bought vending machine chips and ice cream. When my friends and I began to drive, I joined in to eat pizza and submarine sandwiches, with little regard to where my sugars may have been. I was more concerned about controlling who knew what about me than I was with my patterns of caloric intake, exercise and insulin. I especially did not want boys to know what I was dealing with.

As an adult, I have every kind of monitoring device available, but as a teen, I hated being different. I hated God, I hated my body,

I hated being reminded that I had to eat conscientiously. At home, the family would sometimes eat a dinner that was not always allowed on my diet. Lots of fat and starches, common in the 1960s, could include bread, potatoes, butter, gravy, ice cream, and Tastycakes. I was skinny when first diagnosed and needed to gain weight, but heading into puberty, I wanted it all. I remember sometimes crying at the dinner table. My mom came up with a great solution. She told me that anytime I wanted, I could eat my portioned meal in the living room with a tray table watching TV. I thought she was a genius. Those meals became fun. (I still figured out how to get rid of the beans.) Mom even salvaged and washed TV-dinner trays and used them for my meals,

Through my teens, I did not accept invitations to pajama parties. I was so embarrassed that somebody's mom would need to help me eat right and take my insulin. I was invited to go on vacation a couple times with other families, but giving up my modicum of control scared me. It was easier to say no. When I was around twelve, I joined the Girl Scouts. My mom knew the leaders, Mrs. Hecht and Mrs. Mallonee. Those ladies were so kind, and I felt safe in that setting at meetings. When the opportunity came up to go to Camp Illchester in nearby Howard County for a weekend, I panicked. I could not do it. Again, Mom came through for me. She went on the camping trip with our troop. We had a huge cabin for sleeping. Longtime neighbor and friend, Maureen Quinn, was on the top bunk, and I was in the bunk under her. In order for my mom to go, the ladies all drew straws to see who would sleep where, as room for adults was limited. My mom drew the short straw, so she slept on a picnic table—all so that I could go camping and she could give me my shots. In the 1960s, there were no disposable needles and syringes. She brought a little cook pot, the same one I think she had used for my braces wax, and boiled my glass syringe and needle at six o'clock in the morning so I could get my insulin and eat with everybody else. I remember her waving me into a smaller room, where only a few moms were sleeping, pulling up my sleeve and lickety-split, that needle was inserted and off I went.

Having s'mores around a campfire was another hurdle for Mom and me. But she had figured out my food exchanges so that I could eat two graham crackers like everybody else, but with half a sugar-free chocolate bar and gross but real-looking marshmallow cream she had found in a diabetic cookbook. I was so uncomfortable about these rules, but all I wanted was for everybody to think it was the real thing. I wolfed it down just so nobody would know it was not.

Self-control, weight control, and mind control were all essential for me. I did not want to have diabetes, but I did not want to die. Some rebellion by cheating on my diet, drinking beer with my high school friends, and experimenting with marijuana ensued. I discovered that alcohol and pot could lower my sugar, allowing me to eat more. If I didn't think about it, maybe diabetes would go away. If I didn't tell anybody I should not be eating pizza at midnight, then nobody would think I was doing something wrong or dangerous. I'm sure all teens with diabetes go through the same thing. It was a major learning process that continues today. However, monitoring devices and pumps make life almost normal for diabetics these days. Going through puberty meant that my hormones were not cooperating with my eating habits. I gained weight. I had pimples and oily hair. My nose was huge. I grew too tall. Control was going to be my only route all over again. And of course, control that crept into all parts of my life was inevitable.

Many people tell me that I would make a great school administrator. I probably would, but I would be way too much of a control freak. It comes with the territory of monitoring chronic diseases. As a teenager, I often wanted to control situations and relationships with friends and classmates. I sometimes judged people in my head. I was jealous if others were included in something I was not. I wanted to be included so badly that I allowed other people's happiness to dictate my own. But trying to buy a friendship with false compliments or gifts to please the other person does not work. I also care too much about what people think of me. I would not be able to evaluate other adults and be responsible for assessing their job performance. I do much better as a teacher leader, not a principal.

When I became an elementary school teacher, I really could run the show. However, delivering information does not mean that the students are absorbing and processing the information. Readers here, as well as those who have followed me on Facebook, know that I like to run the show, be right, and get in the last word. I admit that. Often viewers of *The Keepers* ask questions and need clarification. Sometimes it gets on my nerves that they have the facts wrong according to the research those of us involved for years have done. It often becomes necessary for me to use active listening and validation of others' opinions in order to keep the record straight about what we know.

I tell people that I tend to be too present in relationships, that it's okay to tell me to back off or slow down or look at things a different way. I addressed this with director Ryan White shortly after I met him. I knew and appreciated that he was the director, but if I disagreed with his interpretation of MY story, I would have to let him know it. He handled me with wisdom and grace, and in the process I learned to take direction. I learned to be quiet and listen. I learned to be a student again.

I work daily on being flexible, approachable, and fair. I want to see theories and ideas different from my own. I am a smart and savvy problem-solver, but I do not claim to know everything; I just act like I do. People see me as a therapist, attorney, social worker, criminal investigator, teacher, big sister, coach, or mom. I'm not any of those things. I know I act like I know a lot, but I am very vulnerable. I thirst for information and strive to excel. I know I am a leader. I know folks rely on me. But I have insecurity and lack a thick skin. I am aware that many men are intimidated by me. I hate that. Probably many women are too. I have a large presence and am very blunt at times. I call it being a bottom-liner, but often I am just so nervous about getting close to nice men again that I likely overwhelm them. I asked my husband once why he was not intimidated by me. His response: "Well, I know how to do dry wall and you know how to spell." He added, "I can't believe nobody scooped you up before I met you." You will meet my Ernie later in this book. I liked that we were not competing and had so much to teach and learn from each other.

I miss being in a relationship with a wonderful man. There have been others since Ernie, but I seem to attract needy men who have a desire to relive their relationships with their moms in the form of a girlfriend that is independent, strong and kind. These guys are usually younger than I am, although not so young that anyone has ever thought the guy was out to dinner with a mom or grandmother. One guy, introduced by a friend, showed up at my home with flowers. First date . . . flowers. Sweet. By the second date he was spending weekends at my house but was entirely too busy to see me in the middle of the week. I soon learned that he was a hoarder—another disease I had never experienced. The first time he took me to his home, we could barely squeeze past the front door. And I was so needy myself that I stayed—for two years. I tried to change him.

The therapist who helped me deal with my husband's death was at first excited that I had found someone new, but the more we talked, the more red flags went up. She finally saw me in the middle of my workday when I managed to get coverage for two hours. When I got to her office, she said, "I'm telling you this as a friend. I think he is an alcoholic, Gemma. The signs are all there." I railed against her, but the more I thought about it, I had to agree. He was a wine specialist for a liquor distributor. He said he was training my palate by having me learn about spirits as we were drinking. There were always spotless wine glasses on his sink drainer, despite all the other junk surrounding it. Those glasses were a precious commodity. When his air conditioning failed, which was rigged up with stereo speaker wire, we spent three days moving all his booze to my cool and air-conditioned basement. I was avoiding the problem, enabling him over and over. But I was a damn good girlfriend.

These guys knew I was able to take care of myself. As soon as it was established in public that we were together at an event, I was left to fend for myself. I was desperate for a social life with a boyfriend and thought I could certainly control the situation. But I often ended up very much alone in a crowd. I voluntarily left each of these relationships. Don't let those men tell you otherwise.

I was ashamed that I was buying into a very bad situation where I was going to be caring for a person who did not care about me. Having been through these messes and come out the other end in one piece, I am now very happy and satisfied with my life. I realize that I am pretty much able to handle anything. I even tried online dating via match.com. That was like having four interviews every weekend. Guy one, Friday happy hour. Guy two, breakfast at Bob Evans. Guy three, ice cream in the parking lot at Friendly's. Guy four, Sunday afternoon at a sports bar. Remember the movie *50 First Dates*? Well, I had fifty first dates but with fifty different men. When one asked me out again, I said no and he asked me why. That was a first. I told him: "I know everything about you, your marriages, your kids, your work and what your house looks like. You know nothing about me because you never asked."

I always offered to split the bill. Only one accepted. I even continued to see him for a while. But he was what one friend called "curmudgeonly." He wrote very sad poetry. He did not want to meet my family or have me meet his. When I realized he sent his teenage daughter out to Christmas shop for me after he saw what I was giving him, I knew this was a dead end.

More than one boyfriend has been alcoholic. That is a disease I knew nothing about. I thought that if the guy was not drinking, there were no problems. Now I know a lot about alcoholism. The anger, the self-centeredness, the need to please me with material goods. Little did I know that I was a chief enabler, adopting the role of the supportive partner. I got so frustrated trying to think of things for us to talk about that might cause my man to ask about me, my friends, my wishes, my goals. It did not happen.

Being in a relationship with a guy provided me with somewhat of a social life. I enjoyed being somebody's person, but I was giving up so much of myself in being there. I was hurt over and over with broken promises and halfhearted attempts at making me happy with a piece of jewelry or cooking a gluten-free meal. One even found gluten-free communion hosts so I could go to communion when we went to Mass. I usually did not want to go to Mass, but that particular boyfriend had a lovely singing voice and I enjoyed hearing him, but that I could do at one of his gigs. I even had a shirt that said, "My boyfriend plays the bass." He certainly did not have a shirt that said, "My girlfriend is a teacher."

I've got this great idea to offer a class at a community college. It would be for men only. They would each pay me one-hundred dollars for one session that lasted ten minutes. If they did not find a girlfriend after the one session, they would get their money back. Here's how that ten minutes would go: "If you want a long-term relationship with a woman, there are exactly two things to remember. Number one is to ask her questions about herself. Number two is to listen to her answers and base your responses and next questions on what she just said." How simple is that? And we ladies, wives, and girlfriends know that it works. I could make a fortune on that class, right?

6

Mom and Me

My relationship with my mother was complicated. She was my greatest advocate and hero, but we did not always get along. I needed her help so much when diagnosed with diabetes at the age of ten, but as I grew up, I felt very guilty at how much she gave up to make my life as normal as possible. In high school, I went through a rough period when I was not emotionally able to give myself my insulin shots. So, every day before school, Mom would come in the bedroom while I was getting my uniform on, and I would hike up my skirt so that she could give me an injection in the butt.

I had been doing well, giving myself needles in the front of my thighs. But with time, that area on both legs began to atrophy, leaving obvious indentations. I noticed this when I went swimming, since my bathing suit would not cover my thighs. The skin there was thinner, so the scar tissue from numerous injections was tough. I decided to wear a swimsuit that was two pieces—a top and a bottom—like a surfer outfit. The bottoms were called *jams*. This worked for a while, but I also had the same atrophy in the back of my upper arms. My cousin, who was diabetic, showed me how to mash my arm up against the wall and inject the area that was bunched up. I became irritable with these body image issues.

I was also, due to puberty, not a fun person to be around, especially at home. I was sad, I was mad, I was disagreeable. I got mad at my mom when she tried to help me because it was not the exact way I wanted help. I talked back. I wept when she offered a new sugar-free recipe for me to try. Meanwhile, there were three other kids in the family. I felt like I wasn't as lovable as they were. I had the braces and the needles and the clothes that did not fit my gangly shape. I had outbursts from my teens into my twenties. When I became a teacher and moved to Bel Air, Maryland, my mom generously spent many days helping me move and get settled. She put together tables and director's chairs, arranged some of her original paintings on my walls and shared my excitement at living on my own.

My mom gifted me a small notebook when I moved out. In it was a section in which she had charted how to do laundry, which items could be washed together, which ones in hot water, which in cold. The next section was how to cook different kinds of meat—chicken, roasts, pork, ham: how hot, how long, covered or not. The last section of that little book, which I kept for years, explained which products to use for cleaning different surfaces. My first weekend in my new apartment, my mother made us sugar-free pancakes, and we sat on lawn chairs on my balcony with trays on our laps.

However, I am responsible for some very trying times, and for hurting my mother. I liked to go back to my mom's house in the West Hills neighborhood where I grew up on my weekends. I would load up my laundry basket and drive the hour "home." There were times when I would be frustrated by my diabetes or my loneliness or my students, and I took that out on my mother. I remember feeling so ashamed but still angry. She would often say, "Gemma, you are an adult now. I am getting too old for you to be yelling at me." She was absolutely right. I learned later that when my mom knew I was coming for the weekend, she would tell the rest of the family to batten down the hatches because Gemma was coming to town.

I spent my birthday once at my mom's house during the first couple years of teaching. I brought one of my dearest friends, Mary Denbow, to join us for the birthday dinner. I don't even remember what set me off, but there was an ugly scene at the table. I got up and walked out of the house, Mary scurrying behind me. We got in the car and, as we were pulling away, she stopped me and said, "Gemma, you can't leave like that. You have to go back and apologize." I did go back in. Nobody said a word. My mom was crying. I hated myself and my behavior. Later that week, I called my mother who was understandably very aloof on the phone. I got angry again, and she finally said, "Hon, I love you, but you need help." As I slammed the phone down on her, I knew she was right.

I was embarrassed that anyone would know I was in therapy—it was not as common as it is today. I don't think I know anybody who is not in a support group or therapy program. To me, now, it's like seeing a dentist but way less painful. But back then, I snuck to my sessions and home again. In therapy, I learned how to deal with the stress of being a new teacher in a challenging school and how to accept my chronic health issues. Mostly, I learned how to exercise self-control and not take my frustrations out on my family. It is a continuous learning experience.

In later years, when I lost my husband, I moved into my mom's house while I was waiting for a townhouse to be built. She was in her sixties, living alone and teaching art in her basement studio. I was an angry mess. Helping your partner to die is a very difficult process, and when it was over, I was lost. I went from being a wife, stepmom, and homeowner to being only a daughter overnight. Two grown women living in the same house when one is grieving the death of a spouse is difficult. My mom was widowed suddenly at forty-nine, so she knew exactly how I felt. But I was selfish. After an argument that I started, I told my mother I hated her. I had never told anyone this before; it is the cruelest thing I have ever said to someone I love. She probably told my siblings.

Therapy, again, helped me repair my relationship with my mom. A social worker who had been helping my husband and me with the issue of parenting my stepson asked a friend of hers, Jeanne Kushner, if she would visit with us. Jeanne spent one of the last mornings of Ernie's life with us. She later agreed to see me as a client. With her guidance and understanding, she was instrumental in bringing my mom and me back together. She also helped me haul myself out of the dark hole of grief and sadness in which I was living.

My mother died in August 2015, a few days after her ninety-fourth birthday. Diagnosed with colon cancer the previous March, her doctor told us that she probably had about six weeks to live. Don't listen to doctors, people. My mom lived comfortably in her retirement home at the Charlestown Retirement Community in Baltimore County for almost six more months. She was not initially in pain; she did not have severe symptoms. She eased out of life with her kids and grandkids and great grandkids around her. We laughed, we cried, we enjoyed our special time with Mom. Because her prognosis did not fit reality, we were never sure what to expect. Mom just kept keeping on. For a while, she was able to be independent in her apartment, even getting dressed to go to dinner with her friends. I went with her one evening. Everybody at her table talked of the weather, the chapel, the games of Mahjong. The elephant at the table just sat there for a blissful hour of no cancer talk. But I saw in their tearful eyes the beautiful love my mother's retirement friends had for both of us.

My two sisters, Toni and Maria, and my brother, Jim, and I alternated each day to come and spend time with Mom. She held court in her recliner, one of us on her bed, watching TV, gossiping about people and savoring every minute. One day, Mom asked me to help her with a task. She wanted me to address birthday cards for everybody in her birthday book, because her lovely cursive was declining. She would sign the card, tell me what message to write inside and then address them. Her inability to do something the rest of us take for granted became an honor for me to complete.

During those months, I decided I needed to have a private conversation with my mother. On Sundays, the whole family would often converge at her apartment, even the new infant, her great-grandson, Wyeth. One Sunday, as we came and went, I waited until only my sisters and I remained. They asked if I wanted to walk to the parking lot with them and, winking, I declined. Mom was in her favorite living room chair, a comfy brown swivel rocker. It was so well-used, that Mom had placed a board and some big flat books under the seat cushion for support. But of course, those were not permitted to show, so it sort of looked like Mom was sitting up high on a little throne. She was just too cute. I told her I needed to say some things to her. (I can't even write this without tearing up, so only a very few people know about this conversation.) I perched on the tapestry-covered footstool Mom really only used to lay her newspaper on if she was not finished with the Sunday crossword puzzle, a weekly pastime she never skipped. And completed within a day or two. I looked at her cute face and her perfectly dyed strawberry-blonde hair, and this is what we said:

"Mom, I have done and said some things to you in my life that I am so ashamed of. I need you to tell me that you forgive me."

"It doesn't matter, Gem. It's all okay."

"But Mom, I feel so guilty that you had to take care of me, and I was hurtful to you.

Please forgive me."

"Okay, I forgive you. But there is something I want to tell you that I have never said before. When you were diagnosed with diabetes, I told God that if He had to send a little girl to Earth with diabetes, I was glad He sent her to me. Because I was smart, and I could read and learn about how to take care of you. I thanked God for you. I always have."

I told my mom how much I loved her. We both cried. I hugged her so hard, kind of like when I was a kid, right there leaning in from the stepstool.

The day before my mom finally died from colon cancer, each one of us took turns telling her we loved her. We wanted to hear her say it back to us. It was funny, and I think she knew that. She must have gotten tired of saying *I love you*. But she said it with each of our names, which was worth more points to us than without our names.

My mom is with me every day now. She knew nothing about what I was doing, that I was investigating a murder and was in a docuseries. I kept it all from her so that she would not worry about my safety. But now, I believe Mom knows everything. She has the answers to who killed Cathy, to who killed Joyce and the others. I know she still worries, but I do think she is proud of what I am doing to change the world for survivors of abuse and to relentlessly strive to find out what happened to Sister Cathy Cesnik.

7

Sister Cathy

My happiest days started in high school. The woman who became my idol opened my eyes to the wonders of books, writing, art and music. Her mark on my life and all those she touched was indelible. Through her, I found myself, my worth, my passions and joys. In the few years I knew her, Sister Cathy Cesnik's impact was profound. Without knowing it, her life and death helped form my beliefs and my teaching.

My Keough school years were good ones for me, full of new friends and becoming my own person. The days in Cathy's class were treasured. Her high standard for us, her students, coaxed us to reach higher. Nobody was ever late to class. Cathy would sweep across the front of the room in her long black habit like a Hollywood actress. The smile on her face was real, there for every single one of us. She bestowed on us her love of writing and reading and acting. We gave it back to her tenfold.

Sister Cathy was different than any other teacher I have ever known. Not because her death made her an icon, which it certainly did, but because she created an environment in which every person in her company felt safe and valued and appreciated. The year I was in Sister Cathy's English class, her name was Sister Joanita. I learned many years later from her family that her name was a combination of her parents' first names, Joseph and Ann, Jo-anita, four syllables.

Her classroom was on the first-floor hallway at Archbishop Keough High School, on the left if you were walking towards the convent from the gym. The desks were in rows from the front to the back, typical Catholic school fashion. I sat in the first seat in the second row. Windows along the far wall of the room looked out onto the courtyard of the U-shaped building. The classroom had a chalkboard the width of the entire front wall of the room. Keough friends, correct me if I am wrong, but I do believe it was an original blackboard, and the teachers had to use bright yellow chalk to make their writing show up. Sister Joanita had beautiful handwriting. You can see it in *The Keepers* in the episode that shows a picture of her at Western High School, where she taught after she left Keough.

Sister always wrote notes and comments on our papers, using our names, which meant so much to me, like this: "Very perceptive, Gemma. I agree with you that Huckleberry Finn's raft symbolizes his journey to adulthood with all its challenges." When she wrote that, I thought I had died and gone to heaven on that raft.

One Monday, Sister Joanita walked in with a large armful of stapled test papers. We had taken what was called a unit test on one of the genres we were studying, or in her words, "exploring together." I figured she had spent the weekend reading and grading all our adolescent bull, trying to figure out how to validate what each of us had to say. We tried to be long-winded to impress her, which usually did not work. Sometimes in class she patiently nodded and said, "Let's get to your point." She stacked the test papers in the order we sat. Whatta nun! As she approached my seat—first seat, second row—she raised one eyebrow. (To this day, I cannot do that, and I really tried to so that my students would get the teacher eyebrow-warning message.) She placed my stapled test face down on my desk. Oh boy, I thought. This is not good. My dad is not going to be happy about this. I waited. But she waited too. My armpits were damp. I lifted the corner of the paper. Across it, Sister Joanita had written, "Gemma, you captured the spirit of the main character in your essay. Please keep writing from your heart. A+." Holy shit. Without moving my head, I peeked up at her sweet face. She gave me a wink and swished on down the row. I would give anything to still have that treasured test paper.

Sister Joanita also expected us to increase our speaking and writing vocabulary significantly. She asked us each to get some kind of little box that would hold index cards for weekly vocab. Most of our moms had recipe boxes, so we had cute metal containers for English class, and mine had spices decorating the outside. Each week, Sister would give us ten new words. The first night, we had to put each word on an index card and find a dictionary definition. Next, we had to find the word's part of speech, and its origin. Then, we had to use it in a sentence, something other than a simple sentence, like, "I have a *melody.*" Or "This is a *conundrum.*" Every year I taught, I expected my students to do the same kind of activity. On Fridays, they would have a combined vocabulary and spelling test. To my students, you know who you are—you had better know how to spell and write using big words!

Another activity in Sister Joanita's class was to bring a new word to school. Once I brought the word *jacktar.* I wrote it on the board and the other girls had to guess what it meant by asking what part of speech it was, trying to use it in a sentence, and asking if it had a Latin root. Nobody guessed that *jacktar* means . . . you know, I'm not going to tell you! Go look it up.

When I joined the drama club, I had very little experience doing anything on a stage. Once, around fourth grade, my teacher nun told me she would like me to be Mary (yeah, *that* one) in a play about Mary appearing to some Hispanic boy and spilling roses all over the ground. It was supposed to be a miracle. There was no way I was going to do this, but my mother told me I should and that she would help me with my costume. My friend, Jackie Torres, said she would be the Hispanic boy. Jackie was, in fact, Italian. We found a cloak to wrap around her while she acted watching sheep or goats in a field, waiting for me to appear. Mom took the plastic roses out of the vase in the dining room, and I took them—plus a big blue blanket—to school for the play. While Jackie was on the stage, I appeared from the side of the stage, opened the blanket and the plastic roses all loudly fell out onto Jackie. I announced some miracle secret thing to Jackie, then the nun told everybody to clap and it was over. The only good part was that Jackie and I got to have bare feet. So, trying out for drama club in front of Sister Joanita was going to be traumatic.

Sister sat in the tenth row in the Keough auditorium. Everybody who was trying out was sequestered backstage in the band room. We were each given a half sheet of paper with a mimeographed reading from a work called "Antigone." It was something about someone named Helen, who I think was a goddess. I read the paragraph. Sister told me not to read the piece but to *be* the piece. Oh boy. I tried to be the piece, which I think just meant I was louder. She finally read the first few lines so I could hear what "being it" meant. Somehow, I got through it and was accepted into the drama club.

Our first production that year was called *In the Season of Hope*. Sister Joanita had written it. It was a choral reading by the drama club members, and interpretive dance by a few girls who had been taking ballet all their lives. The orchestra played some music in between, while the choral club hummed or sang. I guess it was lovely, but I was kind of bored being a choral reader. The dancers had filmy costumes and spotlights. That was the Christmas my favorite aunt, ReeRee, died of breast cancer. My mom told me later that my aunt was so ill that my parents were not sure about coming to the show. But again, they were always there for me, so proud—but that night, so sad. I could see both Mom and Dad wiping their eyes and holding each other's hands. My aunt died the next day.

That year, Sister Joanita and our music teacher, Miss Muffolett, took our class to see the Franco Zefferelli movie version of *Romeo and Juliet*. We had read the play and loved it. So, with parental permission slips in hand, we took a school bus to the Charles Center, near the Morris Mechanic Theater, in Baltimore. I will never forget that afternoon, sobbing with my classmates over the trials and tribulations of the young star-crossed lovers. Coincidentally, it was the same theater, gone now, where Gerry Koob and Pete McKeon, featured in *The Keepers*, saw the film *Easy Rider* the night Cathy disappeared.

We also read *The Scarlet Letter* with Sister Joanita that year. She read the dialogue of Hester Prynne, and if we were lucky, one of us would get to read another character's lines. Since Cathy's death, I have so often thought whether she identified with Hester because of her love for Jesuit Gerry Koob.

The most fun and exciting experience with Sister Joanita was being part of the cast of the musical she wrote called *From Lollipops to Roses*. The musical showcase of songs from movies and Broadway shows focused on young girls growing up. I was part of Group C, which meant that when we had scheduled rehearsals, we would ride the late bus home. On Saturdays, our parents would take turns driving us over to Keough for full and very long practice sessions, but we loved every moment and were never late or sick. One Saturday, both Sister Joanita and our algebra teacher, Sister Ignatius (later Sister Russell), told us we were going to learn a new dance step for the song "June Is Busting Out All Over." For our rehearsals, they wore blue and white plaid aprons with a million pockets. Hiking their aprons and long black dresses up to their knees, they demonstrated the steps together. It was obvious they had practiced together. They had on those nun shoes that are so witchy looking. They ran together down the length of the stage and danced in front of all of us who sat in rapt attention on the steps of the stage. They were so cute and funny; we all laughed and jumped up to dance with them. This was the way they were. Happy, joyful, fun. No hint of tragedy or pain. My group was in the scene called "The Telephone Hour" from *Bye Bye Birdie*. Wearing rolled up jeans and our dads' flannel shirts, we acted out the words to the song, nodding our heads in unison as we pretended to talk on the phone. "Hello Mrs. Somebody, can I talk to Penelope Ann? Going steady, steady for good." The other song that Group C performed was "Tonight" from *West Side Story*. Starting in jeans again and those flannel shirts, the choral club sang "Tonight, tonight, won't be just any night." We disappeared behind wooden sets that the stage crew had built. Our dresses were hanging back there. I was so honored that Sister was helping us zip up and put on fancy shoes. She flew down that row of screens and got us all polished and perfect. Wearing a borrowed pink formal dress and dyed satin shoes from some older girl in my neighborhood, I exited from my screen like a queen. We each held our right arm across our waist and then swept it towards the audience for dramatic affect. The audience reaction was just as dramatic. "Ahs" and "Oohs" greeted our teenage transformation.

The next year at Keough, I had a different English teacher. Because I was not part of the spring drama show, I did not see Sister Joanita as much. Detouring to her room, on the way to other classes was always fun and gave me a chance to say hi and receive her sweet greeting back, always using my name, "How are you, Gemma?" In the spring, I noticed that Sister Joanita was not in school for several weeks. My friend Bruce Weal, who was a student at a local college, arrived at Keough to help with the spring musical. Where was our drama teacher? I heard that Sister had been at St. Agnes Hospital with kidney stones. I also heard that she had a nervous breakdown. And that she had a respiratory infection. Her family has shared with me that they were not aware of her being seriously ill at that time. When she returned toward the end of the school year, I remember clearly going into her classroom after school one day. Other students were gathered around her. We were all in the far corner of the room near the windows. Sister was perched on a desk. When I said, "Hello, how are you?" she turned her sweet-but-wan face to me and shrugged her shoulders. "Doing okay, I guess." I have wondered about this forever. I think Sister Joanita was keeping a lot of secrets to herself. Something was definitely not okay.

In my junior year at Keough, Sister Joanita became Sister Cathy Cesnik. I had joined the choral club, accepted after singing "Wouldn't It Be Loverly" for Mrs. Muffolett, who had gotten married and was now Mrs. Ciaramitaro. So, my interactions with Sister Cathy were again only in the hallway or auditorium or cafeteria.

Our junior brains were on dating, hair, and makeup, and the prom. I had to ask five boys to the prom before one said yes. This is embarrassing (but in the end, I got the best husband in the world, so here goes), they were: Butch Sorbo, Vic DeCesare, Mike Avara, and some guy I do not remember. That experience was really a smack in the head. The one guy who showed interest was Michael Waldner, a cute guy from the neighboring boys' school, Cardinal Gibbons. Right away, on the first date, I got cold feet because I was afraid he was going to kiss me. I told him right there on my front porch that I just wanted to be friends. Duh! So, in the end, my junior prom date was the kid who collected for *The Sunpapers*, Steve Lubyhuesen. I actually asked Steve while I was giving him the check Mom had written for the newspaper. Jeez, I felt like such a loser. It was awkward, but I went. When I thanked him for coming, he said, "It's okay. Now I know how to act when I take Betsy Hall to my own prom."

Over the summer after my third year at Keough, Sister Cathy and her friend Sister Russell left the high school. I did not know more than that they were going to be teaching in public schools instead of at Keough. Most of us accepted it as a part of the social changes that were so frequent in the sixties. I was excited one day when my childhood friend, Jackie Torres, suggested we take a pizza over and visit the nuns at their new apartment not far from Keough. Jackie picked me up, we ordered said pizza from Chiofalo's, and went on our way. I believe it was mid-July, because the nuns, who told us to call them Cathy and Russ, had just moved in. When we arrived, Russ answered the door. Cathy was ironing in the kitchen area. She was wearing shorts and a summer shirt. I think Jackie and I both were stunned to see these two as real people, but they welcomed us genuinely. As we sat down at the kitchen table, Jackie and I looked at each other. Oh no. The pizza box was upside down. Now what? Russell realized our mistake and laughed. Jackie cautiously opened the flat cardboard box. Most of the pizza was stuck to the lid. "I guess we won't need plates," Cathy announced. "Just grab a fork. Let's eat it off the lid."

When we all returned to Keough in September, I was a senior.

Cathy and Russ were not there but nearby, which was nice for all of us and comforting I am sure for those girls being traumatized by the abuse, we learned later, was happening on a regular basis at school. That a one-inch door was all that separated those of us who were clueless from the nightmare happening in the chapel, confessionals, Maskell's office, his bathroom, his car, and the basement still blows my mind. I shake my head in disbelief at what I now know was occurring. He must have spent most of each day grooming or sexually abusing his innocent prey. Boys and girls, children, teens, and adults. The youngest survivor I have met was three when Maskell abused her. The oldest was in her twenties. A monster and his network lived among us. I would not know about any of this until I was in my forties.

8

How Dad Saved Me from Joseph Maskell

My father's impact on my life was not especially evident, even after his sudden death in 1970. My dad had a tough childhood. His own father was an alcoholic, and his mom was ill in her twenties with what was then called "consumption." I think that was another name for tuberculosis. She was admitted to a sanatorium, which in those days was a medical facility for long-term care for people with contagious diseases. I know very little about my grandmother, except that my dad and his brother were left on their own at the ages of fourteen and twelve.

My father lived in the area of Baltimore called Irvington and was an intensely studious young man who worked very hard. He and his brother walked to their aunt's house when their dad left them, off on a binge someplace. His dad's sister, my Aunt Sadie, took them in and raised them with her own children. Years later, Sadie Staub's daughter, his cousin Betty, introduced my dad Charles (Buck) to my mom, Cecilia Kernan. Mom said that Dad was very handsome but very serious. He did not go out, like other teens, because he had a job at the Arundel ice cream store every day after school. I don't like thinking of him having to serve all the kids who came in after school to eat and hang out. Although my dad was pretty much on his own most of his growing-up years, he managed to win a full scholarship to the Mount Saint Joseph High School in Irvington, while my mom was attending Seton High School on Charles Street in Baltimore. Dad walked to school every day, while Mom was likely riding the bus right past him on Frederick Road to get downtown. I bet she watched him through the dirty bus window.

My father, Buck, was in the army during World War II. I looked at a copy of his draft paper a few years ago online. He was stationed behind the frontlines in Germany as an anti-aircraft soldier. His paper said he was in the army for about eighteen months before leaving with an honorable discharge. I guess I thought soldiers in the war were there for the whole duration. However, I do remember him saying he was there during the Battle of the Bulge in Normandy, which is a pretty big deal. Coming home at the age of twenty-six, he and my mom began dating. They married in 1946 and lived with my grandmother, which was not unusual in the 1940s. I think a lot of young couples started out living with parents, who also were the best babysitters. By the time they moved into their own tiny house in Edmondson Village, there were two of us kids and a third on the way.

My father always took a keen interest in our schooling. Although he worked very late hours as a home delivery salesperson for the Jewel Tea Company, he would often ask about homework and what was going on in class. On weekends, Dad would throw footballs to us in the backyard. When he cut down the rosebushes to make more room for running and catching, the neighbors called him

"The Butcher of West Hills Road."

My mom did not drive until after my father's death in 1970, so he was our transportation to baseball games, school play practice, church events and to get cheesesteak submarine sandwiches every Saturday night at Chiofalo's or Mr. G's in Catonsville. Mom would have been teaching art all day, so the subs were a break for her and a treat for all of us. During high school, Daddy also drove us to CYO dances and school mixers. If he picked us up afterwards, I would ask him not to pick me up at the dance but at the closest fast-food joint so that I could walk over there with my friends.

When I entered Archbishop Keough in 1966, my father had begun working for the United States Department of Defense. Stationed at Fort Holabird in Dundalk, Maryland, Dad began working regular hours. However, his trip to and from work through the Baltimore Harbor Tunnel made his day long, but at least he was able to eat dinner with us, get involved with the "Mothers Club" at St. William's, and participate in events at Keough.

Unbeknown to me at the time, his involvement with my high school education and extracurricular activities was critical in protecting me from a monster. My parents came to every show I was in when Sister Cathy oversaw the drama club. Dad would take turns with other parents taking us kids to practice on Saturdays. If he came to pick us up early, he would sit in the back row of the auditorium and watch us on the stage under Sister's direction. On the way out to the car at the curb, he would give my head an easy swipe and say, "Good job, Gem."

During my last year at Keough, my dad suggested we take part in the Father-Daughter Freshman Orientation. I was surprised but very excited. We pored over a map of the school and practiced our parts. It would be our responsibility to take a group of incoming students and their parents on a tour of the school. At each stop, my dad and I would take turns reading or telling them about what went on in that room or program. I remember this so clearly because my dad and I were having so much fun. I know he made some mistakes, but I was not going to correct him in front of new students. I wonder how many freshmen ended up in the auditorium when they thought they were going to the music room. Or who went to the senior lounge thinking it was for all the students. And there was Father Joseph Maskell standing guard at the chapel, looking over the new class of girls. He made my skin crawl, and I know I stepped a little closer to my father at that stop.

My father died suddenly exactly one week after my high school graduation. He and my mom were enjoying a Saturday evening "New Members Welcome Party" at the Hunting Hills Swim Club, where we were members. He and my mom were in the clubhouse laughing with friends. My mother went downstairs to the ladies' room. Suddenly, as someone was telling a joke, my dad fell backwards onto the concrete floor in the clubhouse. He was having a heart attack. Unfortunately, because this was a public place, none of the doctors on the scene were willing to work on him. A Keough friend, Dottie Norton, just last year told me that she was there and got in her car to go get her father, Dr. Norton. The Nortons lived just a few minutes away, and Dr. Norton came to the pool immediately. Although he worked hard to save my father, it was already too late. At his age of forty-nine, I unexpectedly lost my dad and buddy to a massive coronary attack.

I never realized until I delved into the crimes of Joseph Maskell and Neil Magus and some of the nuns who were complicit, how his role as my father at school kept danger away. My dad was visible and involved at Keough. Both my parents attended events. But if Joseph Maskell was preying on girls who may not have been so lucky as to have their dad or mom there on a regular basis, my sister and I may have been approached by the devil. Now I know that, because of my parents, he would never have had a chance. My dad saved me from Joseph Maskell. Thank you, Daddy. I love you.

The Butcher of West Hills Road

Daddy cut down the rosebushes
Shortly after we moved,
The neighbors called him the butcher
Because they did not approve.

It never really made sense to me
Why they all made such a fuss.
One of them had a nasty dog
That barked and scared all of us.

The next guy up, old Mr. Jones
Put nails and broken glass
Atop his fence to keep us out
When balls rolled in his grass.

So, Daddy made a safer yard,
For even when it snowed,
where we could play and run around
Our butcher of West Hills Road.

The moral of the story is
A rule that's not so hard,
When someone cuts the roses down
Please look in your own back yard.

9

Tell the Teacher

My teaching career was a long journey of wonder, success, disappointment and some regrets. With Sister Cathy as my role model, I was an overachieving workaholic. I thrived on my experiences, good and bad, as an elementary teacher. With an outspoken, larger-than-life personality, I made friends but also some enemies. Most of my students grew into happy productive adults. Some did not. What I considered my gift for teaching was often honored, but also challenged and resented by some of those in authority.

After graduating from Archbishop Keough High School, my mom, widowed at forty-nine, depended on me to be her adult person at home. My father's very sudden death threw me into a new role. He was one of my best friends. My dad, Buck, who had fought hard for his own education as a child, was so proud of me: the first in our family to enter a university. Now he was gone. My mom needed me to be the adult with her. I did not plan for any of that. I wanted my dad back. I wanted my teacher back.

Because of my diabetes, I was worried about living away from home having to deal with my health alone, so I made the decision to attend a local university, Towson State College. The summer Daddy died, my mom thought she was pregnant. The stress of his death caused her periods to completely stop, throwing her into early menopause. But for a few months she thought she was going to have another baby . . . at fifty.

In August, Mom rented a cottage in Hyannis Port in Cape Cod and took me and my younger siblings, Maria and Jim, there for a vacation. Dad had always done the driving and Mom had not relearned, so it was my job to get us all there safely. I felt hugely responsible and very nervous. But Mom got a Triptik mapped-out route from AAA, and we loaded up the big red Ford Galaxy 500 and off we went. That trip was important for several reasons: it gave us a chance to be away from the pool where Dad died, to see a new place, and to impress upon me how much my mother depended on me. That was a bittersweet week, I think, for all of us.

We walked along our beach, and one afternoon unintentionally ended up on the beach belonging to the Kennedy family (yes, *the* Kennedy family). No fences or barriers, just their beautiful home set back from the water. I can still picture the dome of their indoor pool. I'm sure if we had not turned back, someone would have come running with dogs and guns and black suits to see why we were there. It would have been alarming and exciting to be accosted for trespassing by the Secret Service. When we took a boat tour the next day, and the captain pointed out the Kennedy compound, we all looked at each other and started laughing at what we had gotten away with. It was also the very moment that the boat started shuddering in rough water and I got seriously seasick.

Returning home, it was soon time to prepare for school. I never saw my college until the day I arrived there. I know! How weird is that? A Keough friend, Paula Brach, whose mom had worked in the school office, ventured with me around the Baltimore Beltway to begin our college careers as commuters. Orientation was a whirlwind, but at least we got to go home at the end of the day and eat a meal each of our moms had fixed, instead of cafeteria food.

I loved college. I met some wonderful friends there. But, because we all lost touch, it was not until the release of *The Keepers* that we all reconnected. I call them my "new old friends." Michael and Teri Helms. Jim and Paula Wissmann. Phil Vallee. Jim Lupinek. Bob and Cathy Fabian. Getting together several times in the last two years has been meaningful and important to me. They have been engaged and supportive of my work on the docuseries and on my journey to help survivors of sexual abuse.

I graduated from Towson State in 1974. I was fortunate to have a job waiting for me in a newly built "open space" school in Harford County, Maryland. The principal, Jack Potter, and the area supervisor, Hunter Sutherland, were holding interviews in an unfamiliar part of Maryland. After submitting my application to Harford County, I was invited to come to the town of Bel Air to interview. At that point, I did not feel motivated or interested in driving over an hour to meet the administrators. But I did. I had a folding map in my car, with the route marked in yellow highlighter. I left my West Hills home and drove through the city of Baltimore on Route 1, taking me through some rather dicey areas. I headed out Bel Air Road to the green rolling fields of Harford County. I can still picture the signs I passed and the cut-off into Bel Air that I almost missed in Benson. Pulling into the old Board of Education building on Gordon Street, I was hot, wrinkled and had to pee. My car had no air conditioning. There were no parking spaces available, so now I was hot, wrinkled, and had to walk two blocks. And really had to pee.

Apparently, my interview with the personnel officer was a success. Within a half hour, he was sending me to meet the administrators for the still incomplete Magnolia Elementary School. This second interview took place at Prospect Mill Elementary School. Nowhere near the new school, I was totally lost. However, when I arrived looking harried, Potter and Sutherland greeted me at the door with big smiles and handshakes. Mr. Potter was the image of Fred MacMurray, so I figured he was a nice guy. Hunter had a southern accent and looked like Santa, sans beard. I immediately relaxed, after peeing of course. Because I had done my student teaching in what was then called an open-space school, I was on the short list for a job at this new school.

Magnolia Elementary was built like a flower: media center in the middle and grade levels circled it, like petals. There were few if any walls dividing the classrooms. Instead, there were large closets on wheels and cork walls that slid open or closed to separate instructional areas, depending on the teaching activity. I had also done a lot of my own artwork to decorate my classrooms. Growing up with a mom as an artist was about to get me a job. There were no art teachers in 1974 in Harford County elementary schools, and Potter appreciated what I had to offer via snapshots of my projects. By the time I arrived back in Catonsville that day, the Harford County Public Schools Personnel Office was calling me to offer me a job and to help me find an apartment. Moving out of the home in which I had grown up meant a first apartment, a new car, and a new job. Exciting but overwhelming.

My teaching career at Magnolia was a learning experience. Potter hired mostly young teachers, many just out of college. The neighborhood of Edgewood, Maryland, was where our students lived. Because the school building was not finished, we had the unique experience of spending the first half of the school year sharing classroom space with the teachers at nearby but overcrowded Edgewood Elementary. The unusual arrangement meant that the Edgewood students would attend school from eight in the morning until noon, and our Magnolia kids arrived shortly after that and were in school from 12:30 to 4:30 pm. We teachers worked in the cafeteria workroom all morning, planning and making instructional materials. When the Edgewood kids and teachers left, we would make a mad dash to their classrooms to set up for our own students. I was so happy to have a job, so none of that was an inconvenience. To me it was fun.

I taught second grade. The first day of my career, I walked across the front of the classroom in my Peter Max platform shoes. I fell over the trashcan onto the floor. The kids loved it. That afternoon, Mr. Potter stopped in to tell me that it was not okay for me to be chewing gum in the classroom while I was teaching. I had a wealth of knowledge about teaching, but these finer points of the art were new to me. No gum, check. No big shoes, check. Oh my, I had a lot to learn.

I spent sixteen wonderful and challenging years teaching at Magnolia. I loved the children and their parents. I had energy and love and lessons to share. Many of the children came from economically disadvantaged homes. A lot of the kids lived with one parent or another relative. Some kids did not have clean clothes every day. But they were resilient and streetwise, with a good dose of common sense. Parents sometimes came to conferences from jobs as security guards, and night nurses. I remember a dad who was wearing a home-monitoring device after committing a burglary. But he was there, and he cared about and loved his son very much. He wanted the best for his child. I was honored to have a conference with him about his son's progress.

We all grew up together at Magnolia. Many of my colleagues are still close friends, and hundreds of my students have kept in touch with me via Facebook. None of them were surprised to see me in *The Keepers*. They were familiar with my personality and all the projects I constantly engaged in with them: Our Mother's Day celebration when my own mother came to school; Bags to Riches trash-bag fashion show; and carnival ticket auctions for good behavior. My teaching years at my first school were rich and varied. Those kids still show me and each other love and support to this day. Those students I had during the time my husband was ill and the year he died hold a very special place in my heart. I hope more of my kids will find me because of this book. You and your families held me up and helped me start to heal. You were a significant part of my journey. Don't ever think I have forgotten you.

I was kind of a badass throughout my teaching career. My philosophy was that if my students were not having fun learning, I was doing something wrong. Thus, many days, my lessons involved singing, dancing, acting and sitting outside while reading. Who remembers the two days a year that we had lunch in the room and then cleared away the furniture so we could skate on pieces of slippery shiny finger-painting paper? And the Halloween I decided we should have healthy snacks and you all cried because you did not want apple cider, graham crackers, and peanut butter? Yes, peanut butter! I let you bob for apples, but you wanted to eat donuts off strings hanging from the chart stand.

When the enrollment at Magnolia shifted, I was assigned to fifth grade. I went to Mr. Potter in tears to protest. His response was that the decision had been made and pointed to the door if I did not like it. As I hung my head like a loser, and rose to leave, he stopped me. "Suppose I give you a class with all the kids you had three years ago when they were second graders?" I almost fell off my platform shoes.

Yes! That year, teaching my kids again proved to be one of my best. Those students are in their late forties now, some even grandparents. But I have found almost every one of them on Facebook or they have found me. (I have begged Ellen DeGeneres to bring us all together on her show but have not heard back from her about that yet!)

Some of you met one of my Magnolia students, Michael Dolce, on *Foul Play*, the podcast I host with my friend Shane Waters. One evening, researching attorneys who handle sexual abuse, I came across Michael's name. Googling him, I saw on my phone my second grader as a handsome, successful lawyer devoting his life to helping others. After I contacted Michael Dolce, I received this letter:

Dear Gemma,

I cannot thank you enough for your note today, though for reasons that would not have been known to you. I remember you, today, as my second-grade teacher. Until today, from my time at Magnolia Elementary, I remembered clearly only my first, third, fourth and fifth grade teachers, Mr. Ayers, Mrs. Bowen, Mrs. Denzer, and Mr. Black. I even remember Mr. Potter as clearly as ever. There is a reason for this gap in my memory. As I have disclosed in public many times now, I suffered grievous, violent sexual abuse at the hands of a neighbor in the summer after first grade, and extending into second grade, as did a friend of mine in my presence. I made no disclosure at the time, and neither did my friend. I kept it all secret, as the abuser demanded from his end of his gun, for 20 years. Without help from responsible adults, my psyche protected me by repressing the memories of those horrific events and even that whole year of my life, through what became decades of terrible, inexplicable dysfunction and fear.

The release of those memories in years of therapy since my first disclosure of my truth has been slow, traumatic and frightening, and nearly killed me a few times, but was also relieving when each memory passed. And I have felt cheated out of the positive memories of that time that were locked away with the horrors.

So when I saw your name today, it was only vaguely familiar at first. But then I looked you up, as the Information Age now allows us to do so readily, and I saw your picture. I recognized you immediately and I wept with relief. The joy of your presence at that horrible time of my life, your smiles, the pure energy and enthusiasm you showed in the classroom, were released and all rushed through me. I am so glad you were there at that time of my life, to provide some happiness to me as a deeply wounded, frightened child. It has bothered me so much all these years that you have otherwise been only a shadow in my memory. That pain was relieved today. So, I thank you for reaching out and providing this to me today. This has been a profoundly healing afternoon for me.

I appreciate too your words of encouragement for the work that I do as a survivor-advocate to heal others and spare tomorrow's children my walk.

I applaud your work for your beloved teacher and mentor. I am so sorry for your loss. I hope that your journey leads you to all the peace that you deserve and honor to the memory that Sister Catherine deserves.

I will share your note with my brother, Joseph. You will appreciate hearing of the path in life to his new name, as he is now known as Linus. After spending years in university science labs, he earned his Ph.D. in physical chemistry from Princeton. He then rejected the ordinary path from there into industrial research, choosing instead to become a high school science teacher. Four years later, he joined a Benedictine monastery in St. Louis, and upon taking his first set of vows, became known as Brother Linus. He has since completed divinity school and become ordained as well as a priest. Together with the monks he lives with, he teaches at The Priory School on the abbey grounds in St. Louis, Missouri. He is very happy.

I would love to keep in touch with you and talk more. My work takes me to many places beyond Florida, so perhaps we could meet also the next time I am in Maryland, if you would like.

Thank you, again, for all that you were to me as a child.

Best,
Michael Dolce

Michael agreed to do the podcast with us without hesitation. You can listen to him via the free Himalaya podcast app. He stoically shared his truth and moved everyone who listened. Michael came to see me at my beach home recently. At lunch, when I asked him how he was doing, he hesitated. With a clenched jaw, Michael told me that shortly after the podcast recording, his son had committed suicide. My heart breaks for him, not only because he lost his precious son, but because his work representing survivors of abuse continues to be his passion, even after losing his own child. Michael and I have agreed to continue to stay in touch. We would like to write an article together, about our work with survivors. I am honored to know this survivor. He is a hero.

A year after my husband Ernie died, I left Magnolia and transferred to a school in another part of Harford County, Jarrettsville

Elementary. Although I loved my previous years, I felt the need to take care of myself and work with students who were not as disadvantaged as those in Edgewood. My years at Jarrettsville were therapeutic and successful. My students were proficient and independent, and their families provided help and support for every teacher. I was very fortunate to be able to spend more time teaching and less time worrying about my students.

The second year teaching fifth grade at Jarrettsville, a child named Joseph Dilello was in my class. Joey was a very sweet child, kind to everyone, and determined to succeed. In 2013, when I began investigating the background of Reverend Joseph Maskell, I happened to read his obituary. Joey's mom was Maskell's niece. Joey had been named after his uncle, Joseph Maskell. Using social media, I have tried unsuccessfully to contact Joe and his mom. He would be in his thirties and likely have his own family. It would be intriguing to ask him how everything that happened with his uncle has impacted him. Joey, if you are out there, please get in touch. You were a kind kid, funny and always smiling.

I was very fortunate to work with some outstanding, fair and reasonable school administrators. They guided me both in pedagogy and curriculum. I embraced new ideas and put new spins on old-but-proven techniques. I realize this is not an Academy Awards speech, but I cannot tell my story without mentioning some of the most remarkable educators who have influenced my teaching. Jack Potter, my first principal, selected a group of very young teachers to become the faculty for a new school—Magnolia Elementary in Edgewood, Maryland. As assistant principals, Bill Alexander and Tom McShane each added uniquely different but equally valuable gifts to new teachers in a very needy school community. Laughter and fun with the families and staff were the norm. I will always remember how each treated me with respect and appreciation.

In 1990, when I transferred to Jarrettsville Elementary School, I was interviewed by teachers with whom I would be working, and the supervisor, Barbara Douglas. That principal, Gerry Mack, was like no one I had ever met. Considered a transformational administrator, he schooled us in Outcome-Based Instruction. The teachers pretty much ran the school with Gerry as our facilitator. I learned to do the same with my students. They were in charge of their learning, and they created our classroom rules, which we renamed "guidelines." We never used the word *rules*. We were a community, a team, which included their parents. When I arrived at Jarrettsville, the only quandary I had was that I had *four* "room parents." Since planning class parties was not my forte, I was delighted. I told the parents to do whatever they wanted in terms of planning for class events.

The strategies I saw Cathy use were again put into place. The Socratic Method, in which she asked us probing questions and encouraged us to explain out thinking, I developed with my own students. A reading strategy call *reciprocal teaching*, in which the students become the teacher in a reading group, made reading interactive. Achievement soared. An energy grant from the Baltimore Gas and Electric Company provided us with a class garden in a fenced-in area once reserved for a portable classroom. A recycling bin soon followed. Experiential learning involved so many integrated subjects— math, science, and reading—that teaching those subjects separately became almost impossible. Within a year, my fifth-grade students were producing a weekly TV show for other kids in the building, featuring jokes, announcements, comedy acts, and interviews with staff members. It was an experience we savored.

One year, a student developed asthma from second-hand smoke. The class began to explore, on their own, how this happens. They investigated what they could do to prevent smoke-related health problems. My students wrote letters, did more research, and talked to adults who smoked. They came up with a plan. In 1992, smoking in teachers' lounges was a normal thing. My students, working in pairs, convinced those teachers not to smoke in the building. The adults agreed. The students then invited local TV and newspaper reporters to visit and cover their project. Several responded, and we hit the airways. The county school superintendent, Dr. Ray Keech arrived unannounced one day in our classroom to congratulate my kids for a job well done. He invited them to the next school board meeting, where they could talk to the public about the possibility of naming Jarrettsville the first smoke-free school in Harford County. I was so proud of them. They arrived at the board meeting in their Sunday clothes with their notes. They took turns speaking and presented their idea. The board voted unanimously to publicly name Jarrettsville smoke-free. That proclamation, now almost thirty years old, still adorns the hallway of the school to this day. The next project we undertook as a school was to participate in the Shuttle (later Space) Amateur Radio Experiment (SAREX), that allows schoolchildren to talk to astronauts in real time via cameras and ham radio.

My life as a teacher brought me immense joy. Healing from the death of my beautiful husband is largely due to the children and families who were part of my life. When a family invites you to dinner, and the kids ask if they can call you Miss Gemma in their home, you know you belong. I belonged. This chapter is dedicated to those educators who have made a huge positive impact on me as a teacher and person. They believed me, and believed in me, even when others did not. Their support and respect never waned. They, to this day, are highlights in my life. Thank you to the following:

Maryland Department of Education
Dr. Nancy Grasmik, state superintendent
Dr. Robert Anastasi, Maryland Business Roundtable for Education

Harford County
Magnolia Elementary School
Jack Potter, principal
Tom McShane, assistant principal
Mary Denbow Sliwinski, teacher
Nancy Charvat, teacher
Calvin Black, teacher
Marian Wilkinson Stewart, teacher
Rita Garrity, teacher
Ginny Wolfkill, teacher
Donna Brightbill Stufft, teacher

Jarrettsville Elementary School
Gerry Mack, principal
Kathy Bem, assistant principal
Barbara Douglas, supervisor
Ellen Tracy, supervisor
Ann Ramsay, supervisor
Sharon Grove, teacher specialist
Courtenay Servary, teacher
Lynn Blom, teacher
Tracy Frey, student teacher
Kim Funk, student teacher

Abingdon Elementary School
Larry Mills, principal
Bev Hibschman, teacher

Prospect Mill Elementary School
Dan Harner, principal
Regina Smidt, teacher
Mary Murray, teacher

Central Office
Christine Reynolds, supervisor
Dr. Ray Keech, superintendent of schools
Albert Seymour, assistant superintendent of schools
Dr. Deborah Heiberger, assistant superintendent of curriculum
and instruction
Dr. Robert Christopher, supervisor
Phyllis Van Winkle, supervisor
Nancy Harkins, supervisor
Paul Schatz, teacher specialist

Baltimore County
Edgemere Elementary School
Chris DuFrane, speech therapist
Kate Hartman Miller, teacher
Sue Capron, teacher
Doris Long, teacher
Kim Nelson, teacher
Leanne Bauer, teacher
Karolyn Mason, teacher
Tony Annello, teacher coach
Lansdowne Middle School
Kiki Geis, principal

Libby Wynkoop, assistant principal
Ken Lockette, assistant principal
Barbara Shields, principal
Jodi Pasquale, mentor
Wendy Prioleau, mentor
Lindsay Morningstar, teacher
Amy Jubb, teacher
Christopher Bunn, teacher
Ethan Huber-Smith, teacher
Sarah Bosworth, teacher

Colgate Elementary School
Kevin Connelly, principal
Lora LeBrun, teacher
Chrissy Snow, teacher
Gordon Michaloski, teacher

Southwest Academy
Karen Barnes, principal
Kim Wadsworth, mentor

Central Office
Mary Jacque Marchione, supervisor
Jean Imbriale, supervisor
Debbie Piper, supervisor

I know this list has given a lot of you something new to think about. Some of you may be surprised to see your names here. Maybe you never knew how much you influenced me as a teacher or friend. Thank you from my heart.

10

Seeing I'm Not Seeing

A fuzzy shadow in the corner of my left eye. What is that? I look away and back again. The movement of my head causes the shadow to move, like the frayed edges of an old movie reel. (I am on a loopy road trip to see people I know and miss, and I'm relaxing on the patio of an artist friend in Roanoke, Virginia. Harriet Stokes, a renowned watercolorist in the South, has invited me to visit her mountain home. Her sister, Frosty, had been my neighbor.) As dinner is served on her lovely lanai, the shadow moves and enlarges. What is going on? Not wanting to alarm Harriet, I keep this event to myself; I am leaving the next day, heading home to Baltimore anyway. But I am scared. Distracted, it is hard to converse with my gracious hostess. But I put my big-girl pants on and get through the next couple days. The moving lines seem to jiggle when I walk, settle when I sit still or lie in bed. Having had diabetes for almost twenty years, I am well aware that eye problems are common.

As soon as I arrived home, I confided in my dear mom, then in her fifties. I made an appointment with an eye doctor immediately. Enter creepy Dr. Gerald Miller at St. Agnes Hospital. He took a look and told me my eye was bleeding inside. Bleeding? The tiny, new blood vessels that diabetics develop as a result of retinopathy were trying to carry oxygen to my eyes. The original blood vessels are lined with plaque, resulting in an obstructed route to deliver oxygen. New but weak vessels form and they leak. The scientific name is neovascularization. The treatment Miller recommended was laser treatment called photocoagulation, which burns the ends of the leaking vessels. I agreed. After one treatment, consisting of about 600 laser beams and a lot of pain, I returned to his office. Laser treatment for this condition feels like somebody is jamming an unsharpened pencil point in the eye. Had the treatment worked? I sat in the examination chair, anxious with anticipation. Feeling vulnerable and not tough. Miller walked in. Instead of looking through the looking machine, he commented, "You have great looking legs. How long are they anyway? Do you have a boyfriend?" My response was, "WHAT?" Totally taken by surprise, I leapt out of the chair, which was facing the closed door. I shoved him out of the way, grabbed the doorknob and ran out of the room. Grabbing my jacket from the coat rack, I yelled to the waiting room, "That man is a pervert! Don't go in there!" Although I never went back, I did file a complaint against Dr. Miller with the Medical Board in Baltimore. I also was able to look at files there, that showed other women had experienced the same treatment. How satisfying to hear later that Miller lost his license due to malpractice.

Needing to find a new doctor, I asked one of my neighbors, also a doctor, whom he would recommend. Dr. Basil Morgan at the Wilmer Eye Clinic at Johns Hopkins saved my vision. Although it was necessary for me to undergo multiple laser photocoagulation treatments, he was able to slow down the progression of the retinopathy.

However, after several years, the leaking inside my eye was so severe that the blood covered my entire eye, leaving me blind in the left side. Following a surgical procedure called a "vitrectomy," the viscous material on which the weak vessels grow was removed and replaced with saline solution. I could see again. The next year, the same thing happened to my right eye, and the same surgery became necessary. Because diabetic eyes age quickly, I was soon faced with having to have both cataracts removed and lenses implanted.

Having unexpected eye issues is very scary. Sometimes, I would have a vessel bleed at school. That is the fuzzy shadow that, in a day or two, can turn into what looks to the patient like black paint that occludes one's vision completely. I had to sleep sitting up, hoping that nature would take its course and the blood would recede by gravity. Thankfully, an observer cannot see the blood, so I did not look like some kind of zombie with dripping bloody eyes. It's all inside, but to the patient (that would be me), it is frightening and stressful.

I was extremely stubborn and relentless trying to find answers. The cataracts were minor compared to the retinopathy. In those days, Dr. Morgan was permitted to give me the cataracts in a little clear jar of alcohol that I could take to school to show my students. One cataract was brown, one yellow. The kids passed the sealed jar around. Some asked if they could do science reports on why the colors were different. Without any more encouragement, my class did research, interviewed their grandparents who had the same surgery, went to the library and became experts in cataracts.

As a young person, I tried to hide my disability. My husband, Ernie, would never let me walk alone through a store because I had limited peripheral vision. Laser treatment destroys rods, responsible for night vision, and cones, which help us determine colors. Scar tissue forms from the photocoagulation, scars which cannot be removed.

I would trip over little kids, trash cans, parking barriers, and my own shoes, which were always all over the house. In my classroom, I talked animatedly, striding around the room, waving my arms for emphasis. More than one kid had to duck to avoid being whacked inadvertently in the head. I got very good at scanning, turning my head from side to side, almost as well as that girl in *The Exorcist*. I reminded myself of my Gemma doll with the rubber head.

Presently, as I am writing this chapter, one of those cataract lens implants is dislocated due to age; it's been in my eye for thirty-five years. Because repairing it is risky and unpredictable, I am weighing all my options before making a decision. The vision in my right eye is like looking through a partially frosted window. When you meet me, if it is dark or dim, you will notice that I carry a huge Maglite that lights my way through crowds. I might ask you if I can hold on to you or your husband, if he is cute. I'm not going blind. I'm quite fixable (I am followed by not one, but three awesome ophthalmologists), but I need to find the time and the right doctor to do this. I don't want to mess up my schedule for fun and hanging out with you and other people who have offered to help me right wrongs.

Two years ago, I had to give up my driver's license because I could no longer pass the vision test. I had a new car, a place to go to every month at the beach, and now I could not drive. This was overwhelming for me. I grieved this loss intensely. It took me months to figure out how I was going to live without wheels. But, you know, I am resourceful. I figured it out. My family and friends rallied. When the day came to turn in my license, my sister, Maria, accompanied me to the Department of Motor Vehicles. I was nauseous and afraid. I had to tell the nice counter lady that I was surrendering my privileges to drive. Then I handed her my license. She showed me where to go to get the picture that goes on an identification card, which the government tries to make look like a license, but it doesn't really. I have often wondered if other people who had to go through the same process look like they have been crying in that stupid picture. So, get this: I have not missed driving for one second. Once I got used to the idea and figured out how to work around it, life was easier. I live on a bus line and, as a senior citizen, can ride for two years for just seven dollars. I also walk everyplace. I have a grocery cart that I drag to the store. I push it home, while people yell, "Hey Gemma!" from their cars. You can yell if you see me; it's kind of fun. My friends here are great about taking me to appointments and shopping. And Uber Philis is now my regular driver. She bends over backwards to get me where I need to go and stays with me until I am ready to go home. I am blessed not to be able to drive. My drivers feel good, I feel lucky, and we all benefit.

Vision problems have followed me for many decades. Knowing I could go blind, I refuse to feel helpless. Seeking treatment and wanting immediate results is frustrating for me—asking for help is not my style. Wondering why this was happening to me was in my head a lot. I am not a martyr or a soldier, but I am a determined hardhead who works diligently to beat this shit. I did not know until many years later that a young Hopkins doctor told my family it might be a good idea for me to learn Braille. Had I known at the time, I would have smacked that man. I did not learn Braille; I learned how to fight.

11

As Much As Much Can Be

Ernie: *Gem, how much?*

Gemma: *How much what?*

Ernie: *How much do you think I love you?*

Gemma: *Hmmm . . . I don't know. How much?*

Ernie: *As much as much can be.*

Gemma: *Hey, hon.*

Ernie: *Yeah?*

Gemma: *How much?*

Ernie (grinning): *How much what?*

Gemma: *How much do you think I love YOU?*

Ernie: *How much?*

Gemma: *As much as much can be.*

This became our private dialogue any time we needed to hear it. Either one of us would start. We had the script memorized. It was our thing. In the car, in bed, in the hospital, on the phone. As much as much can be.

Meeting my soulmate was a delightful surprise. My husband, Ernie, was my best friend. Our short time together is a love story of learning, sacrifice, and joy. I found a new Gemma, a woman who was funny, sensual, and loved with everything she had. But it was also a very sad time for us, grieving his coming death together. Never taking a moment for granted, we were able to capitalize on our time and shared energy, and the life we built together. Ernie's spirit remains with me always. He is my guide; I turn to him in good times and bad. He never lets me down.

This chapter is composed of entries from our private journals. Some of mine are written as short stories. Our lives were a lot of short, very precious stories. I've never shared these before.

THE CRAB FEAST

The crab feast in August 1984 was our back-to-school get together, so getting Ernie there didn't just happen. I had been hearing about him from my friend, Mary Denbow. She had invited him to dinner at the apartment she and her boyfriend, Steve, shared. They had also gone to Ocean City with him for a weekend in July. Well, I thought I'd like to meet this nice guy. In fact, he had been living in the apartment Steve vacated when he went to live in sin with Mary. He was a sign-painting artist. I even considered calling him under the premise of asking for help with the lettering I was painting on a friend's truck. Ernie Hoskins' signs, Steve told me, were all over Bel Air businesses, including Steve's own company, Bel Air Carpet. After Ernie's death in 1989, I repainted that one, up on a ladder. It was more for me than for Steve.

Getting Steve to bring Ernie to the crab feast seemed like a simple solution, right? Simple? Never. The guys would come together and meet us there. Upon arrival, there's no Steve, no Ernie. Mary gets her guy on the phone immediately. "Where ARE you guys? I'm here. Gemma's here. You are NOT here."

"He forgot. He went to his mom's for dinner." Mary told Steve to call Ernie at his mom's house and get him over there immediately. Because I thought this was a blind date, I had those butterflies. I kept making excuses to go out to the car. Getting CDs, getting a jacket, getting nervous. I wanted to do the introductions outside so that nobody would know that we had never met before. This was getting complicated. Finally, after my third trip outside, I spied Steve's car pulling into the parking lot. Okay, here we go. And there he was. Tall and lanky, cut-offs and a gray sleeveless sweatshirt, flip-flops. I told him years later I hated that sweatshirt, but he did look awfully cute. (And I wore those cut-offs for twenty years.) The beginnings of a beard were evident. And those eyes—so brown and dark you could not see the pupils; so deep, even I had trouble looking in them. "Love eyes," I called them later. Love eyes. My first look at the man who would become my friend, my lover, my husband. The man I would love deeply and lose tragically four years later.

As they strode toward me, butterflies turned to full-on nerves.

Before Steve could introduce us, I of course poked out my hand and said, "You must be Ernie. I've seen your artwork. I'm Gemma." Nothing like overwhelming the poor dude. He obviously had no idea this was a setup. But I took him under my wing, guiding him to the beer and grabbing seats at the long picnic tables. He told me about his son, Eric, then seven and in the second grade. I suggested he might want to bring Eric to the aquarium in Baltimore (where I just happened to be a guide).

As the evening drew to a close, I thought perhaps Ernie would invite me out, but no such luck. He told me later he had no idea I was supposed to be his date. Men are dumb sometimes. Later that week, I asked Steve if Ernie had said anything about me. "Yes, he said you were funny." My response was, "Funny weird or funny ha-ha?" Steve replied, "He did not specify." Oh boy. I guess that's the end of that. But weeks later, I got up my nerve and called that nice man. His phone rang. And rang. And rang. Not giving up, I sent Ernie a postcard of the aquarium and invited him and Eric to come on a tour with me. Bingo. I was a second-grade teacher, so it was no news to me that his kid would love this date. And Eric did. I remember watching them at the seal pool from the window above on the appointed Sunday. My guide friends gushed at Ernie's cuteness.

Weeks later, he sent me a thank-you note with fish on it and invited me to dinner. For a while, I thought he assumed I had money. I had dated very little, had never really had a boyfriend, and here he was, a sweet, kind dad who was movie-star handsome. My life was about to change.

THE DATE

The doorbell downstairs rang at my apartment on University Parkway in Baltimore. I yelled into the intercom that I would be right down. Isn't that the way all the living-in-the-city stories start? I had spent the better part of several evenings deciding what to wear. What I thought were brown pants were actually purple, a yellow shirt with a gold vest and a black blazer. All covered up, very layered and very not feminine. I was terrified. I couldn't believe this guy had asked me for this date two weeks ahead of time. Who even does that? Well, he did. When the elevator opened into the lobby, there he was, in layers too. Gray jacket, V-neck sweater, button-down shirt with a tie. A *tie*. Wow. And that full beard with those dark eyes. Yowzah. I did not want to screw this up and have it be the first and last date with this cutie. My hands shook and my belly lurched. We exited the building, and I prayed somebody would see us, and that I would not fall down the broad cement steps. I was already worrying what would happen when we came back. Should I hug him? Ask him in? Oh my.

Rounding the building into the church parking lot next door, I was relieved that he had not been ticketed. The Christian Scientists did not like us parking in their lot. Often, if I parked there, a locked chain would greet me when I came out to go to school in the morning. I figured out how to get out but did not want that to be necessary tonight. Getting into his dark blue compact something, I detected that new-car smell and grinned. Ernie told me on the way to the Rusty Scupper that he had bought the car that week just to take me out! He didn't think I would go on a date with him on his motorcycle. I think I would have walked to the restaurant just to spend time with him.

It was so hard for me to make eye contact with Ernie as we sat opposite each other in the upstairs bar waiting for our table. He was disarmingly sweet, kind, humble. He guided me through the packed bar to our table. Wanted to know about me. Me? I remember sitting across from him eating and talking and laughing. I remember ordering pasta with shrimp and pesto. It could have been peanut butter on mashed potatoes, and it would still have been the best meal I have ever eaten in my life. I was smitten.

The evening ended with me inviting Ernie for a drink at Phillip's in the Baltimore Inner Harbor. He accepted. I was so pleased to see two guys I had gone to school with working behind that bar. One nodded; the other winked at me. Walking across the harbor to the parking lot near the National Aquarium, I wondered why Ernie did not take my hand or even touch me. Did I smell like garlic? I asked him about that months later. He said later he was afraid he might scare me away. And I was thinking that my connection with the two bartenders was scaring HIM away. When he took me home, I did not have to worry about asking him in. He asked me if he could come in and use my bathroom. Awkward, but of course. I kind of stood in the entryway so I would not listen if he made noise in there. I worried that I might have left my underpants on the floor and a bra on the doorknob. Leaving with a smile and a thank you, he sort of brushed a peck on my cheek. But there was so much more to come.

SAD DISCOVERIES

What began was a year of unexpected highs and lows. As we got to know each other over the next several weeks, Ernie shared with me that a year before we met, he had fallen from a telephone pole while working for Comcast Cable. Having kicked himself in the groin with his work boots, he reported to the company doctor immediately in severe pain. He was shortly sent to a urologist. When that doctor told him he needed to see an oncologist, Ernie decided he would do nothing.

All this occurred before I even met him. His first marriage was very troubled. Ernie told me that his former wife had been unfaithful. He said she also emptied their bank account of all but two cents. The house he had just built himself went into foreclosure. Ernie was permitted to see his son only on weekends. He did not have much to live for. So, when he shared with me that he had fallen and I saw the damage for myself, I told him that either we found out what was wrong, or I was going to leave. This was so difficult for me, setting an ultimatum, but I already was so in love with this man, that I could not imagine being without him. I grew up in a family of strong women who want to know what we are dealing with. After taking a day off from my teaching job, Ernie and I met with a new urologist who told us that the problem was likely a blood clot in the right testicle, which by that time was the size of an orange. Seriously. I can still see us sitting in his waiting room like it was yesterday.

Ernie was admitted to St. Joseph's Hospital for outpatient surgery in January 1985, a few short months after our first date. His mom and I waited. And waited. Hours went by. This was not good. Because I was not Ernie's wife, the surgeon would not talk to me, but he took Ernie's mom, Nellie, aside. She then took me into the hospital cafeteria, bought me a coffee, and made me sit. I did not want to sit. There was something strange on her face. Then she told me that there was a tumor. The surgeon had to remover the entire right testicle and vas deferens.

The floor fell out from under me. It was a gut punch. Nellie and I held on to each other tightly. I sat right down on the floor at the phone booth and called my mom. I was devastated, but Mom talked me through how to get up and go in his room. Nellie had asked me not to tell Ernie that it was cancer until more testing the next day was completed. At the same time, I was being treated for diabetic retinopathy, and a new bleed started that afternoon, probably from crying and stress. What looked like black paint to me occluded the vision in my right eye almost completely.

I only remember sitting and holding his hand while he slept. I was alone. I was his person. How would we survive this? I never once thought about leaving this man who was now my life. With a sad but grateful heart, I looked up to see our friends, Mary and Steve, come through the door. I had prepared them ahead of time about what was going on. I know they were there for me. We did not talk of tomorrow. But when they left, Ernie asked me why he was not allowed to eat. I told him to call his doctor, who was by that time at his own home. I watched my person stoically receive the news. He even thanked his doctor. He looked at me and said, "I have cancer." "I know, hon," weeping softly. It was so hard to leave him, but when he finally dozed off, I crept out and cautiously drove home, seeing with only one eye, down Charles Street, remembering our first date on that very same avenue. Entering my apartment, I was greeted by my sisters, mom and brother. I was enveloped in their arms and hearts. I had no idea how they got in. I did not care. I needed them and would continue to need them in the months to come.

How lucky was I to have found Ernie and that we loved each other unconditionally and completely? My heart was full of him but breaking at the same time. I never once thought of being anyplace else, regardless of what was ahead. We belonged together forever, but forever did not happen.

Transferring from St. Joe's to Johns Hopkins Hospital a few weeks later, it was determined that Ernie's testicular cancer had metastasized in the year since his fall from that damn pole. Now we learned we were dealing with lung cancer. Six months in and out of the hospital was our new normal. I was also having numerous eye surgeries, for the retinopathy and for cataracts. Sometimes, our doctors arranged for us to be at Hopkins at the same time. Ernie walked with his IV pole across the hospital to see me. If he beeped, there was always a doctor or nurse to the rescue nearby to reset his pump. The grin he wore coming in my room was the highlight of every day. Often in gym shorts and a hospital gown open in the back, he had no idea how cute and sexy he was to his girlfriend with a patch on her eye like a pirate.

Ernie and I both loved to write. We wrote cards and letters to each other throughout our whole relationship, even when we lived in the same place. Being an artist, his were always adorned with cartoons and sketches of us, together and alone. Although I have had other relationships since his death, nobody has ever treated me this way. Put me first. Loved me intensely. He is the only man who ever told me he loved me before we even thought about making love. To me that is huge. Sex is so easy, so casual. Love, and telling someone you love them, is not easy and should never be.

Our life together was wonderful and horrible. Health issues followed us constantly. After being in a coma for a week following a very intense round of chemotherapy, Ernie had to relearn how to walk. The day he was released from the hospital, his mom took him and his walker to a jewelry store where he bought an engagement ring for me. His family sent us to dinner at our Rusty Scupper spot, of course, where he proposed.

His bald head and no eyebrows attracted rude attention of course, but he was alive. We were together. Getting up to go to the restaurant's salad bar, he hesitated so I could go first. Returning to the table, there was a diamond looking at me from my water glass and a waitress grinning ear to ear. Ever the logical one, my first comment was, "This is beautiful, and the answer is yes, but both our cars need new tires." I know, right? The next day, we joined his siblings for an Orioles game at the stadium in Baltimore. I flashed that stone all over the place. When some idiot called him "Mr. Clean," a dig at Ernie's baldness, my usual rude remark back was stifled. Nothing could ruin this day, and I do not even like baseball.

Over the next year, Ernie's health improved, and soon we were making plans for a wedding. He returned to work, this time, not on poles but in customer service. His doctor, a wonderful man named Ross Donehower, felt confident that the cancer had been arrested. Both he and my eye doctor from Hopkins, Basil Morgan, attended our wedding on August 6, 1986, at the lovely St. Mary's church in Pylesville.

Our family friend, Reverend Jack Kinsella performed our ceremony. It was real. It was us. A down-home country wedding, with stinky cows in the fields and moose heads on the walls of the Jarrettsville VFW Hall. It was catered, of course, by the Ladies Auxiliary. Real roast chicken, not rubber; real mashed potatoes, not instant. I think Mom and I argued over the plastic utensils, but they were the nice, heavy kind that you do not throw away. A DJ played the wrong song when we came in, but there was so much fun and laughter and family joy. I paid Eric, who was eight, to wear a tuxedo without complaining. Although the pants were way too short, he gladly accepted my forty bucks to be good.

We spent the next year happy and excited. We bought a house, a fixer-upper in the old part of Aberdeen, Cal Ripken's hometown. We got to work, restoring the house to its original appearance, with Victorian gingerbread trim and a clawfoot tub. I learned to use tools. Our cottage was taking shape.

GEMMA'S JOURNAL, SEPTEMBER 11, 1986

Well, here I am a married lady, with the nicest sweetest husband in the world. Being Mrs. Hoskins is fun and funny at school. Most teachers get married in the summer, I think, so that their students don't have to make a huge adjustment.

Going home after school is the best part of my day. Sometimes Ernie and I are pulling up in front of our little Victorian cottage on Edmund Street at the same time. We bought the tenant farmer's house that was part of the Edmund estate in the old part of Aberdeen. I am learning about tools and wallpaper. I get to hold the drywall ceiling up while Ernie shoots the nails in. I'm tall, so maybe that's why he married me—to help with renovations.

Wallpapering, I have discovered, is an art. My job is to hold a flashlight sideways to determine if there are any wrinkles. I occupy myself while holding the flashlight by singing Beatles songs. Ernie joins in. We sing Beatles songs in bed at night holding hands. We take turns picking the song. My favorite is *If I Fell*. He likes *And I Love Her*. We rattle off our "How much" mantra before we go to sleep.

I want to pinch myself. Is this a dream? Is this a fantasy? No it's real, and it's really me. I found the best person ever. Sometimes, in the evening, when I am watching out the window for Ernie's car to come around the corner, I want to cry, just from love and knowing he will be here soon. He shows up with an unexpected bunch of flowers from the lady on the corner. He tells me that flower lady is getting to know him. I tell him that if she is pretty, she better know you are taken. I'm still really so insecure about myself with him. I scare men. I asked him why I did not scare him. He said it was because I know how to spell, and he knows how to do drywall. That totally makes sense to me. We are not competing. We need each other. He needs me to encourage him to follow his art passion. I need him to tell me to slow down. We honor each other.

Every year I get an original painting from Ernie for Christmas. I guess while he was home recuperating, he was very busy painting, and making Hamburger Helper for us for dinner. He asked me once if I had any idea how many flavors it comes in. I did not even want to know. Our favorite dinner is pancakes and sausage. Forget the Hamburger Helper.

Ernie's son Eric visits us on weekends. I care very much about Eric. He and his dad have so much fun together. But I worry about Eric; he has seen his dad ill way too much. Today they are making walking sticks with beads and feathers. They've also created beads and feathers on safety pins for my sneakers. We are so weird sometimes.

GEMMA'S JOURNAL, SPRING 1988

Ernie had a seizure at work today. He has a brain tumor. I am numb. All the way home in his parents' car, I cried. All the way. Tomorrow, we will see Dr. Ross at Hopkins. We are staying with Ernie's parents tonight. Neither one of us slept at all. Just held hands and cried.

ERNIE'S JOURNAL, JANUARY 1988

Today I'll start writing in this journal. It's an average day. Today, I'll do the laundry, wash the dishes, watch TV, and vacuum the carpet. Very boring. Drove to Fallston Hospital this morning for blood tests. Only two days before I have to go back to Hopkins for five days of chemotherapy. I only got sick a couple of times last month, and the IV went in on the first try. I weigh 188 lbs. right now and have about a half-inch of fine hair, which I hope to keep. Dr. Donehower said he will increase the dosage this time because I tolerated the last one so well. I feel good about this course of chemo. I have so much to live for and to keep me busy. School, remodeling the house, Gemma, Eric, walking sticks. No time to worry about cancer.

Gemma is my life. I'll write that many more times in this book, I expect. She is my best friend, my partner, my business secretary, my sparring partner, my teacher, my lover, my chauffer, my travel companion. She is everything I live for. Without her help and guidance, I would have died two or three years ago. I owe my existence to her. And if I am allowed the long and happy life I know lies ahead, I'll owe that to Gemma too. I love that woman. And I pray to God to accept my treatment and to overcome the obstacles that stand in the way of complete recovery. I need her, and I know she needs me. Thank you God, for Gemma.

ERNIE'S JOURNAL, MAY 1988

I feel really good today. I'm in the air-conditioned family room as it is ninety-one degrees outside. Gemma and I put a contract on a four-acre lot on Day Road near Street, Maryland. It was listed for fifty thousand, but we offered thirty-five. The owner accepted our bid. We went to take another look at the lot, and as we were leaving, he said, "I like you guys. I want you to have it for thirty-two." We are calling the new homestead "Days End."

I want Gemma to learn how to shoot a rifle in case anybody tries to trespass. She doesn't like the idea. At all. We also started landscaping the Aberdeen house. It's hard work and slow, but we will get there. Gemma had this idea of getting in the wheelbarrow and having me push her around the yard. I did the same. We laughed our heads off. We locked ourselves out of the house a couple days ago. I was able to stand on the top edge of the back screen door and get in through the bedroom window. Gem held it steady while I climbed up from the deck railing. I must be getting stronger. School is out in two weeks for Gemma. No chemo for the last couple months. So glad to get a break. Hair is starting to grow again. I'm tired of being bald.

ERNIE'S JOURNAL, JANUARY 20, 1989

I'm finishing this book here. Even though I wanted to express my feelings as I was undergoing chemo, I think it ended up as a bellyache book. To complain about aches and pains. And my spelling is as terrible as ever. Still, it does express what I felt during part of this past year. I won't throw it out, but no one may read this as long as I am alive.

GEMMA'S JOURNAL, FEBRUARY 1, 1989

I am lying on the couch with my head in Ernie's lap. An oxygen hose is helping him breathe. We are talking about his death. He has left me a list of what he wants for his funeral: closed casket, pine boughs on top. He wants to be dressed in his new jeans and the flannel shirt I just gave him for Christmas. He has insisted on his good hiking boots, the new ones, because he has no idea where he is going to have to walk. His dad will get the old ones, he tells me. I ask him, through tears, if he will let me know what heaven is like, and he says he will if he is allowed to do that. He asks me to see the Grand Canyon for him. I will. I tell him how much I am going to miss him. We are thirty-five years old. He says, "Gemma, listen to me. The time we have here on earth is like a grain of sand on a beach, compared to the time we will have together in heaven. I will be waiting for you."

The Saturday before Ernie died, Father Jack Kinsella, who had married us, came to spend the afternoon with us. Ernie asked for privacy with him. This is what resulted from that visit. Ernie asked Jack Kinsella to read this at his funeral.

In Ernie's words:

Let everyone know that I am at peace with myself and with God, that I am not afraid to die because I know Jesus will be with me. I look forward to the time when we will all be together again.

Please pray for Gemma, our parents and our families. Please pray for all of our friends. Please let them know how much their prayers and support have meant to me and how that support kept me strong. You will need to give each other strength now so that you can live on, go on with your lives. I'll be waiting to see you again.

My Ernie left this earth on Ash Wednesday, February 8, 1989. His energy is dispersed throughout the universe. His impact on me and my life continues to this moment and evermore. The heart really does go on, and true love never dies. I received more love in the few years we were together than most people receive in their whole lives.

And as he requested, I saw the Grand Canyon for him. I crept to the edge and threw in a tiny photo of his beautiful face. I learned, through years of therapy and reflection, that helping him to die, that giving him permission to leave me, and letting him hear me say that I would be okay was likely the most painful but also the most honorable thing I ever had to do. And I learned that, because I did not drown or waste away, nothing else ever in my life would be that hard. I was not going to be afraid. Ever again.

Seeing Stars

A backyard field, a July long ago
Long away from city lights
I think I saw the stars.

A warm sweet man by my side
A worn soft quilt
He pointed to the sky and said, "Look, Gem."

And then my eyes went starless from
Laser beams and bleeding veins,
A rods and cones new language
For me to learn.

Then he was gone, the stars went out
I could not see the stars.

I try so hard today . . . tonight.
I think I see one, mine, out there.
But then I quit;
It's not time yet.
I cannot see the stars.

12

TOY 1992

I was not going to drown. I was not going to die. Grieving my husband's death became more of a search for meaning rather than a deep dark pool. Some days I felt like it had all been a perfect dream. Then a nightmare. But I kept waking up to it being reality. Grief is the kind of pain that is very nearly physical. My chest and heart and gut literally felt hollow, my head and brain numb. I would get up and mechanically do whatever needed to be done. Putting one foot in front of the other was often an effort. A lot of you know what I mean—losing a spouse is uncharted waters for most of us. My way of dealing with Ernie's death was not the ideal way, I will tell you this right off the bat. But at the time, it was the only thing I could think of. I was thirty-five, people. I was not supposed to be a widow at thirty-five. However, I wish I had handled some things differently.

I became involved in everything I could fit into my week, often just to fill in my time. I told myself I was honoring Ernie by trying to help other people, but it was really so that I would not have to think about what had happened, where I was, what I was thinking.

Meals on Wheels, a sexual assault hotline, and teaching art after school filled my days and kept me from having to think too much about myself. There was a lot of avoidance, some denial. But very normal, I know.

About a year and a half after Ernie's death, I decided to change schools. I needed to put my own wellbeing first and felt that I could not be at my best with so many kids needing extra help at Magnolia. After careful consideration and several interviews, I accepted a position at Jarrettsville Elementary School. The house Ernie and I had lived in while I was at Magnolia was less than a block from my new school. Again, there are no coincidences.

To my surprise, during my first year at Jarrettsville, the assistant principal nominated me for the Harford County Teacher of the Year Award. Initially, this was a very awkward situation for me. I had been in the school less than a year. But the selection team that interviewed me for my position teaching fifth grade was made up of the grade level teachers with whom I would work. They made the decision because, as Gerry Mack told me later, they were the ones who would have to put up with me. So, they made the choice to hire me. A very forward-thinking school. That team became my friends and teaching partners. Lynn Blom, Linda Webb, and Courtenay Servary absolutely know how much I valued our relationships. I needed to know that they were okay with my nomination before accepting it. They were all on board and supported me through the process. When I was selected as the County Teacher of The Year, my team celebrated with me. Subsequently, a few months later, representing Harford County, I was honored to be named the 1992 Maryland Teacher of the Year.

The experience afforded me, my students, and their families a rich year of attention and adventure. We visited the governor in Annapolis and were honored on the floor of the Maryland General

Assembly. We were visited by TV and newspaper reporters. Because I was not on leave from teaching, I took my students to as many events as possible. For other events, Mr. Mack provided the same substitute teacher, so that my students got very used to having two teachers that year. I met with the parents of all my students to explain what would happen and answer their questions. They pitched in with gusto. One mom typed all my correspondence, another worked with my students as an extra teaching assistant. One dad, a draftsman, did all my charts and posters in his perfect script. My years at Jarrettsville were exciting and rich with learning experiences for me and my students. I appreciate all of you who made that happen for us.

After two adventure-filled years, I was offered a central office position as a teacher specialist, under the direction of an area supervisor. It became my responsibility to provide professional development and coaching to teachers in the area. Although I missed my children terribly, I felt this new role teaching adults was the right next step for me. Under the tutelage of supervisor Dr. Robert Christopher, the teachers in our schools excelled. We were an effective team: Bob presented the theory and development of a new strategy or curriculum, and I would then show the teachers what it looked like in the classroom with demonstration lessons. The students in our schools met or exceeded the state standards in testing during those years. The teachers embraced and internalized effective practices. Our six schools became a learning community for sure. I cherished working with every one of you.

Unfortunately, during this time, jealousy raised its ugly head and challenged my integrity and reputation. Bob decided to leave his supervisory position and became the supervisor of grants for Harford County. Math wizard and business guru, we knew he would be successful. I was reassigned to a different supervisor with other schools.

Her last teacher specialist had ended up in the hospital due to stress. The first time we sat down to plan, my new boss said to me, "I want you to know that if I don't like something you are doing, I will tell you." Thus began one of the most challenging years of my career.

The teachers enjoyed working with me. I helped them not only in planning and management but also in grading papers, making teaching materials for them and running errands. I had credibility with them because they knew I was still a classroom teacher. The new supervisor, however, resented my initiative and knowledge. That I had also been named the Maryland Teacher of the Year created friction between us. I attended meetings at the state level. I was involved in state educational committees and task forces. As a result, I was asked to do more and more menial tasks to keep me in my place as subservient to her position. One night at ten o'clock, I was awakened by a call from the supervisors' office. I could hear the copy machine in the background. What the heck was this about? My boss, on the other end of the line, told me to prepare something for the following morning's meeting at one of our schools. After several hours, I completed the task. Rising early to make the copies of the project for sixty teachers, I arrived at the designated school. My supervisor then asked me to bring materials from her car on a cart for the meeting. During the presentation, I noticed that my prepared materials had been moved to the exit door. At the conclusion of the session, I asked about sharing the information I was requested to prepare the night before. The response? "We don't have time. They can pick it up on the way out if they want it." Another time, I was instructed to prepare a math presentation. Arriving at the school, I noticed another teacher setting up a math tutorial similar to mine. My supervisor casually commented, "Oh, I asked somebody else to do it. You might learn something from her."

I finally reached my breaking point. After the Harford County Assistant Superintendent of Elementary Schools arranged for me to assist a human resources specialist from the central office, I was directed to be the facilitator for monthly school-improvement team meetings. Now I was doing two jobs. Having designed a schedule that would work for everyone, I presented it to both offices. My area supervisor reprimanded me for doing it without her. I finally lost my temper and told her she had control problems. She retorted by telling me she would have to report me for insubordination. And she did. At the end of that school year, I learned that I would have to apply for my job all over again. On the day of the interview, one of the secretaries stopped me on my way to that appointment. "I need to tell you something," she said. The last time she said that was to tell me that my earrings did not match, which is not unusual for me, but this time her tone was subdued. "I think you should know that you are not going to get your job back. One of the supervisors told me last night that none of them want to work with you." Choking back tears, I put on a smile and entered the interview room. Ten frozen smiles greeted me. With grace under pressure, I answered every question with articulation and knowledge. I imagine some of those individuals are reading this chapter right now, so I am taking the high road and not repeating any names, but they know who they are, and they know what they did. And I could tell you a whole lot of dirt on many of them. But to them and about them, I will say, "I never lost my integrity, I never lied, I never put any of you down. Well, maybe one of you. You deceived me out of jealousy or conceit." And I want to say to one of the most interesting and quirky ladies I ever met, Nancy Harkins, that I knew you were not involved in that scam. I want you to know that, when you called me the next week to see how I was, I honored and appreciated your integrity. I left that job and those bizarre people who kicked me out. I took a classroom job where one of my dearest friends taught. My Abingdon fifth graders blew the lid off the state assessment that year. I knew how to teach them to be independent learners who thought about thinking. It's called metacognition. You lost; I won. My kids won.

I then spent another successful year working in technology around the county for my dear friend and colleague, Phillis Van Winkle. Phillis was also an outsider, never really buying into gossip or gang mentality. She was her own person. We did good work, focusing on school improvement, not on who was better than whom. We were proud of the work we did, creating an environment in schools where teachers and their students learned about technology together.

Subsequently, I was offered a position as a teacher mentor in the Baltimore County Public School System. When I walked into the Harford County Human Resources Office and handed my resignation to the secretary, I said clearly, "I quit." And I do believe I flipped the bird to the supervisors' office as I flew down Main Street in Bel Air in my new Jeep Wrangler.

My job as a mentor, working with new teachers in one school started out as a dream. Edgemere Elementary School became my new home: wonderful teachers who were craving ideas and support, and a principal, Mrs. X, who recognized that I had a lot to offer and provided me that opportunity. Many dear friends were made there.

I was at Edgemere the day of the 9/11 attack on the United States. My officemate Chris and I clung together. Busy with delivering kids to their waiting parents, we were on autopilot, not crying until the end of the day. Chris is still my very close friend. Little did I know how much I would need her; she kept me keeping on.

However, at the beginning of my third year at Edgemere, something changed. Something seemed different at school. From the beginning, Mrs. X often asked me to stay late, helping her with the School Improvement Plan, professional development, or assistance plans for struggling teachers. I agreed enthusiastically. But I was exhausted with the thirteen-hour days and an hour ride to and from home. There was no stipend for this overtime, and it took its toll on me. The same year, I also had a boyfriend. I had gotten cosmetic eye surgery during the summer, and I had a life outside of school. I was no longer willing or able to stay at school until eight with no food or consideration for that life. Mrs. X was not happy with me.

I was given odd tasks to complete. She asked me to find out if the teacher in the classroom above her office had the office bugged because the teacher always knew what was going on. (The teacher knew what was going on because other teachers loved her spirit and encouragement and often talked with her.) Another day, Mrs. X told me that she was going to be interviewing for a new maintenance man. She said she had to make sure it was somebody who would feed her information about the teachers. I knew this was not right but kept it to myself.

One day after she had been away at a meeting, Mrs. X called me to her office and asked why I went through her files while she was gone. She was standing in the dark looking at her partially opened file cabinet drawers. I was stunned. I did not have keys to any offices or file cabinets. What was going on?

The principal asked me to begin sending her my weekly schedule every Sunday night. If I was not at the location on the schedule at the exact time listed, I had to answer for my discrepancy. For a mentor, things change daily. A teacher could be sick, or a music event would impact a planning session or demonstration lesson. I could not win. Teachers with whom I worked could opt to have me in their rooms when they were having a formal observation. For most teachers, I was a comfortable encouraging presence. In the middle of one first-year teacher's observation, Mrs. X told me to leave and not to attend any more observations. I could not do anything right.

In the middle of March, I was called into the principal's office. Her assistant principal sat stone-faced in the corner. Mrs. X took a sheaf of pages from under her blotter, announcing that she had been collecting data on me. Collecting data? What followed was two hours of criticism, supported, she claimed with made-up and taken-out-of-context statements. She accused me of calling the parents in the community "white trash." My mouth flew open. I had never used that term in my life. My parents did not raise me to be a bigot. Then she claimed that I was not nice to certain teachers, that I never smiled at them. In actuality, I was one of the most welcoming faces at that school. I enjoyed many fine relationships with the families in the community. Next, she said that I spent too much time in certain teachers' classrooms. This principal had already sent all these charges to the Mentor Management Team in the Central Office, who would be conferring with me.

I do not remember how I got home that night. I took the next two days off, claiming an earache. I cried a lot. I could not understand what was happening and why. The second day off, I wrote a rebuttal. Returning to school, l left a copy in the principal's office and sent copies to the mentor supervisors. I could barely put one foot in front of the other I was so sick. During this year, I began to show signs of malnutrition. My muscle mass disappeared. My legs were so swollen that I could not bend my knees. A few months after the incident with the principal, I was diagnosed with celiac disease. Mrs. X stood in my office door and told me I looked like I had cancer. I weigh 145 pounds. I am not a small person, but during that period, I lost 25 pounds. This was a life-threatening situation. In 2003, celiac disease was difficult to diagnose. I was dying. And my condition was exacerbated by the stress imposed unfairly on me.

My diagnosis coincided with the end of the school year. I was told by the principal and the mentor management team that I was not needed at Edgemere. I went to TABCO, the Teachers Association of Baltimore County, which represents the teachers in contract issues. Mentors are the same as teachers in terms of seniority and salary, but because I wasn't being dismissed from the system, TABCO could not help. My evaluations had satisfactory ratings, but the narratives that accompanied the ratings were not. As long as I had a job, there was nothing I could do.

I was given several schools from which to pick an available classroom teaching position. But the members of the mentor management team had also been colleagues with Mrs. X, so nobody believed me or they were afraid they would be next. It occurred to me that I was the scapegoat. If she could get rid of the Maryland Teacher of the Year, anybody was fair game.

Principal Mrs. X left the Baltimore County school system suddenly and without notice during the following summer. A friend with connections shared with me that it was because of the manner in which she treated me and several other teachers. A few years ago, I insisted that my record be cleared, and it was. The office of Human Resources was compassionate and cared very much that my reputation was not sullied. On the last day of school, one of the women in the mentor office who had judged me so harshly offered me a position on the other side of the county, again over an hour from my home. She told me that this would give me an opportunity for a new start where nobody knew me. I graciously thanked her, hugged her and went on my way. And then I threw up in the parking lot. Next to her fancy car.

I transferred to Lansdowne Middle School, where I spent the last seven very happy years of my career. I mentored wonderful teachers and enjoyed my work with young teens in a diverse population. My administrators, Principal Kiki Geis, and Assistant Principals Ken Lockette and Libby Wynkoop appreciated my skills and experience. The next principal there, Barbara Shields, was the only Catholic nun running a public middle school in the state of Maryland. "Sister Janet" was smart and fair. The students tried to get sent to her office so they could see her strange dolls dressed in black dresses with black and white headpieces. To this day, Barbara Shields is one of my best badass cheerleaders. Working with my colleagues Jodi and Wendy, we were able to increase teacher effectiveness and student achievement.

I have wondered, but not very often, what those who did not value what I had to share think of me now. I know now that they were threatened by my expertise and ability to work more effectively with teachers than they ever could. Are they happy? I don't think so. Were they ever? Probably not. They never moved up in position, so I guess they retired disappointed. Not me. I've never been happier. Those who gain satisfaction by hurting others are usually very sad and petty individuals. I wanted to forgive them, but I have not been able to do that. I have never embraced the Oprah thing of forgiving someone to set yourself free. I've tried. It doesn't work for me. I'm happy and free and they really don't deserve my forgiveness. In fact, you know what? I used what I learned to bite the bullet and move forward. They did not. Their rusty old wheels have not moved them far. But me? I'm good. I keep on keeping on.

13

Making Things Happen

Being acknowledged for my teaching career was both an affirmation of Cathy Cesnik as a teacher and a personal achievement. Striving to give my students and colleagues as much of myself and my expertise as possible, I began to assume a professional development role in my local school system. Doors opened. Opportunities arose.

One year, I thought it would be cool to collect soda cans and have a recycling project at Magnolia Elementary. Every grade, K through five, began collecting cans in huge green recycling bags. By Friday afternoon, there were at least fifty bags of cans. We would take them to the recycling center in my teaching partner's truck. By Monday morning, all fifty bags were swarming with ants. The sugar in the sodas drew thousands of those critters. Screaming, we dragged the bags to the parking lot and onto the truck bed. Itching and smacking, we drove the cans to the recycling center and onto the belt. I still do not know how my buddy Nancy managed to get all the ants out of her truck. But she was an adventurer and never complained.

Another time, I had an idea for Valentine's Day that we could collect and donate items for a soup kitchen in Baltimore, Our Daily Bread. Called "Jarrettsville Has a Heart," the project was organized by our fifth graders, collecting specific items picked by each class: toothpaste, toilet paper, paper plates and cups, deodorant, combs and brushes, canned goods and drinks. On Saturday, the Jarrettsville community parents all showed up to transport the supplies. Kids and parents and teachers made the one-hour trip to the city, where the volunteers at Our Daily Bread were waiting. It was such an easy thing to do, no money collected, no permission slips, just boxes and boxes of needed items. It's rewarding to show kids how to make things happen.

Knowing I had been through tragedy and turmoil and survived, I grabbed every golden ring. I thrived. Continuing my education via travel, scholarships and stubbornness, those choices also defined me. People knew me. They asked for me. I answered.

I retired from Lansdowne Middle School in 2010, while I still enjoyed my job working with new teachers and struggling teachers. I had the opportunity to teach kids and adults. That is the best time to retire, when you still like your job but don't want to do it every day. As soon as I retired, the Baltimore County Office of Professional Development gave me the opportunity to spend four months mentoring in a school as a substitute for a mentor on extended maternity leave. At the same time, I was invited to periodically train other mentors. I was able to see that my teaching and mentoring skills could change the climate of classrooms and schools. I loved my life. When the mentor returned, I spent the rest of the year living with friends in New Zealand. I wrote curriculum while I was there, and when I returned, had a newly approved course for mentors and department chairs, *Mentoring the New Teacher*. My classes filled quickly. I could see change and internalization of the course objectives. Since my retirement, I have traveled to both New Zealand and Australia alone. I've had the opportunity to live and work with teachers in foreign countries. Taking chances, experiencing every opportunity, has convinced me that my life is a learning adventure.

I know that my leadership skills and initiatives have given others the chance to make things happen as well. I am pretty fearless. I speak up and speak out. During my year as the Maryland Teacher of the Year and after, I was proactive on state-level committees that were making a difference. Membership on the Maryland Business Roundtable for Education put me into the arena of businesspersons who were interested in what was happening on the front lines. I welcomed being a voice for other teachers. Talking about their accomplishments gave individuals outside the school systems a look at the inside. Perhaps I was naïve, but I volunteered ideas for change and was often invited to lead those changes. It did not occur to me that some would see me as a threat. I did not see myself as a threat, but as a catalyst for positive change. I utilized my contacts and resources to enlist assistance for teachers and students.

I rarely struggle making decisions. And I have never done things halfway. Changing schools, moving residences, and speaking up or out are opportunities for me to grow. I like to throw pebbles in a pond and see the ripple effect. I thrive on change. I love to meet new people, like many of you. When I make a decision I do not back out. My pride and determination move me ahead, or behind in some instances. Not looking back, completing a task or journey is how I roll. If I want to take on a new challenge, I do it wholeheartedly. The only challenges so far that I cannot finish are driving a stick-shift and touch-typing (I type with all the fingers of my right hand but just the index finger of my left. I look at the keyboard not the screen).

I have always loved to learn. Learning to draw as a kid was a no-brainer. Mom had classes in the basement on Saturdays, so we all got to go to art class for free and she did not need a babysitter. Years later, as an adult, I wanted to learn watercolors, so my sister Maria and her husband, George, welcomed me into the adult classes at the Staub Art Studio. You saw their art school in the first episode of *The Keepers*. It's next to the Caton Tavern, where I have been slammed by viewers for drinking wine and hitting on the owner. Laugh your heads off. I had fun and helped create a film that changed the world. I make things happen.

PART THREE

Keeping On

14

Social Studies

I credit technology for much of what has been learned about the murder of Sister Cathy and all of what has been learned about the sexual abuse at the hands of Joseph Maskell and those with whom he was associated. Through Facebook individuals and groups, websites and online research, communication with thousands of people willing to help around the world has been possible. However, in the same way, if social media, cell phones, and the internet had been available in 1969, I doubt there would have been a murder of a nun who was trying to save her students. Cathy would have had a lifeline to rescue her. Her GPS could have shown us where she was. She would be here.

If technology today was available all the way through the horrific career of the pedophile monster Maskell and his network of thugs, politicians, clergy, cops and businesspeople, our survivors could have taken pictures, recorded voices, screamed for help that would have been heard over the phone by family and friends. If smart technology had been available in 1967, Charles Franz would have a record of the trip his mom made to report abuse to the archdiocese. If it had been available in 1965, the boys abused at a summer camp by Joseph Maskell and William Simms could have contacted someone for help. And the Roman Catholic Church in the Archdiocese of Baltimore would never have been able to cover up what these pedophiles and murderers did to our friends. We are smart women and men. Look what we have accomplished in the investigation over the last six years because of technology—more than was gained in the previous fifty years of pain, death, agony and continuing abuse.

Let me also say, however, that Facebook is toxic. People post comments on group and individual pages that they would never utter in person because they would be decked. Two Keough pages were the basis for our grassroots investigation, and since then a number of new pages have come and gone, or come and not gone. Through these pages, I learned that a troll is a person who likes to trash others on social media, sometimes using their own name, but usually hiding behind fake accounts and made-up monikers. I've seen screenshots from pages with illustrious names like The Truth Seekers, The Truth Finders, Debunking The Keepers, Abbie and Gemma The Lesbian Tribute to Mary and Jesus. Seriously. I could never make this rubbish up. I have sometimes tried to join these groups, which is very humorous because the moderators scramble to batten down the hatches and block me, which I had already done to them immediately after asking for membership. I admit it has been fun to see roaches run.

Overall, the internet and social media has brought the world closer. *The Keepers* was released in 175 countries in 25 languages. Presently, there are 125 thousand members on the Netflix-owned Facebook page, The Keepers Official Group. This is the first and only time in my life that everybody in the world agrees about something. Not the Kennedy assassination, not 9/11, not any election or war has garnered the worldwide support for survivors of clergy abuse. Only the Roman Catholic Church still refuses to be transparent about what has gone on for centuries. The first time director Ryan White filmed me in my home, I said straight into the camera, "I believe this secret goes all the way to the Vatican." I still do believe that. I guess the Pope knows who I am because of technology, and I assume he has seen *The Keepers*, I have written several times asking him to give me a call, but I guess his cell phone can't get a good signal where he is. Funny nobody else has trouble reaching me.

I would not survive were it not for my phone and more than 100 apps. I do everything with my phone: monitor my health, pay bills, correspond, investigate murders, write books, check FB messages and texts, tweet, play games, listen to books and music, watch interrogations on YouTube. You don't want to mess with me and my phone. No way. But I also realize that it is an addiction that is a double-edged sword. Strangers have hacked my accounts and gotten into my emails. People I know have created secret pages and websites to attack me. I have several individuals who will, at short notice serve as my drivers and bodyguards. I asked Ryan once if he thought I was in danger because of all the social networking and publicity about this story. His response? "The more public you are, the safer you are. Besides, if somebody kills you, at least we will have a good idea of who and why." Some comfort, Ryan.

Books are written about the impact of social media on society and mental health. All I know is that it has opened doors of communication to those of us who want to communicate and find out who killed Cathy. However, those doors would never have been closed in the first place if social media existed fifty years ago. My love-hate relationship with social media continues, but my struggle for people to like me because of it does not.

15

Surreal Tsunami

The Keepers was released in May of 2017, all seven episodes at once. None of us who were involved saw it before the world saw it. After watching the trailer at least a hundred times and ruing my hair and imperfect make-up, I watched the series over the course of about twenty-four hours. Having been filmed regularly over the course of two years did not prepare me for what was to happen next. Within a day, I received Facebook messages from all over the world. Like hundreds each day. In many languages. There is a translation button on FB that allowed me to see what everyone was saying. Warm wishes arrived from every European country, Canada, South and Central America, New Zealand, Australia, and every single one of the states in the Union.

Because I was very sick with a cold for several weeks after the release, I was confined to bed, but still able to read and respond. I have written to every person who acknowledged our work. The messages were of three categories: new information, congratulations, and stories from abuse survivors. My apartment was quiet and still.

Just Teddy and me. But outside, the world was sizzling with the story.

My life turned strange. Everybody suddenly knew me. I had a person to keep track of what I was doing, saying, wearing, writing. I was given lessons in how to answer questions and deal with the media. I made mistakes. Lots of mistakes. People loved me, hated me, wanted me, wanted me to go away. I knew this was part of the story, and because I had met similar challenges as the Maryland Teacher of the Year, I embraced this newness and held on tight. This was a roller coaster. None of it seemed real to me because it literally happened overnight.

One of the first days I felt up to taking an extended walk with Teddy, a young woman on a bike in the middle of the street, screeched to a halt and fell off her bike. As I approached to help her up, she screamed, "Mom! Mom! It's Gemma! It's Gemma and Teddy!" I was happy to oblige with a selfie. I had no idea how many selfies I would be asked to do. In restaurants, people would send over drinks, pay for meals, ask for more pictures. One evening, a woman approached me in a restaurant and asked if she could hug me. She cried while telling me that the courageous women of *The Keepers* had given her the strength to come forward about her own abuse at the hands of a priest.

The tsunami was not always positive or productive. I was criticized on social media and by people I thought were friends for showing off, seeking fame and fortune. I still to this day have not taken a penny for my work on *The Keepers*. People in documentaries do not get paid. We all did it because we care and because it was an important story to tell. At one point during that summer, Netflix graciously sent me a hundred-dollar gift certificate to Phillip's seafood restaurant in Ocean City. On the evening, I took my family there for dinner, several of the servers, young men and women in their twenties, recognized me. They politely asked if they could have a picture with me. Because I believe that being public gets our story and mission across, I obliged. When the photo showed up on Facebook with the caption, "Thank You Netflix, for dinner and fun," all hell broke loose. I was banged around for accepting the gift card. Criticized and called salacious for posing with five young men, and then "bragging" about it. I was so naïve about being a public figure and so unused to the attention, positive though most of it was. I was stunned and very hurt at the reaction. And by the way, that hundred dollars covered half our bill. Aunt Gemma gladly paid the other half, happy to be with family.

In the middle of the summer, I began to receive threatening messages in the middle of the night from strangers with common names, like John Smith or Mary Jones. No offense to those nice Johns and Marys, but the only way I could deal with it was by blocking every John Smith and Mary Jones on Facebook. Do you have any idea how tedious that is? Messages saying, "You killed Sister Cathy. Now it's your turn" and "We know where you live, so don't wait up for us."

In July, producer Jessica Hargrave called me to ask if I would appear with Abbie on the television talk show *The View*. I agreed immediately. This would give us a chance to clarify what we were doing and answer questions. Abbie was more tentative, but if you have not seen that episode, she nailed that interview and I invite you to witness her finesse. We flew two days later to New York, where Ryan White and his sister MacKenzie met us with open arms. I remember sitting in the lobby with Ryan while he took a call from somebody in New York, setting up a meeting for the next day. To our surprise, when he turned his phone on speaker, we heard the voice of Dr. Ruth Westheimer telling us how proud she was of what we had accomplished. Her life story was the next project for Tripod Media. *Ask Dr. Ruth* is a poignant and artistic documentary about the life of this very precious lady.

The View was a unique and interesting experience for us. We had to arrive early at the studio, to meet with the producer and for hair and make-up. I agree that Abbie and I looked good, but if you spent ninety minutes with professional stylists, you would too. I was nervous because I do not see well in dim settings. There were backstage halls to navigate and a waiting area below the stage where we stood until we were to go onstage during a commercial. My buddy Ryan never let go of my arm until he handed me over to someone who put us in our seats and miked us. We knew what the questions would be and had gone over answers with Ryan and the producer already. However, because this is a live show with a studio audience, the questions and answers are often changed based on the responses. Nevertheless, I think we did a good job. I think we got the message across that the church in Baltimore was not being truthful about the abuse that had been reported fifty years ago when Cathy was murdered. I remember commenting that we estimated there were, at that date, at least one hundred women and men who had come forward to report abuse by pedophile Joseph Maskell.

Returning home, I received an email from one of the archdiocesan attorneys "congratulating" us and reminding me that all adults in Maryland are mandatory reporters. He wanted me to know that he assumed I had reported to the police all one hundred of those who had come forward. My response to him was that I did not have to be told. I had been a mandatory reporter all my adult teaching life. Additionally, those reporting abuse had all already reported on their own to the police. I won that round, dude!

After our appearance on *The View*, I asked publicly to meet with Archbishop Lori in a neutral place to talk about the situation in the Catholic Church and how we could maybe work together to change things. My suggestion was to meet in a park or on a playground, where we could swing on the swings or have sammies on a picnic table. My treat. He could wear jeans and a t-shirt, and we could have a reporter document our meeting. No response. No meeting. No kidding.

Numerous interviews by phone and in person followed the release of *The Keepers*. And always I would ask them to contact my Netflix person, who would either tell them no or ask me if I wanted to do the gig. If I did, she did not leave me hanging out on the phone alone with the interviewer. She silently listened, ready at any moment to get me out of a sticky situation or tell the interviewer that I was unable to answer a question that involved confidentiality. Memorable individuals with whom I spoke include movie reviewer Sister Rose Pacatte, a Catholic nun. I love Sister Rose; she is a badass like me but won't admit it. Nancy Grace was also a very kind woman who felt very deeply that the Sister Cathy case was a disgrace to the Catholic Church. I enjoyed our conversation immensely. Local radio host Clarence Mitchell IV ("C4") always makes me feel welcome and valued. Michael Gerlach of *Focus on Disabilities* did several radio shows with me and some of the survivors so that folks could understand better PTSD and the damage that sexual abuse causes. My WMAR-TV friend, Christian Schafer, became a true advocate. Not only was he always available to take my calls or answer my emails, but he tried to cut through red tape to get files and records for us that had been in the possession of former assistant state's attorney Sharon May. Denise Koch from WJZ-TV was also available numerous times to the women of *The Keepers* and others not ready to reveal their identities. Later, Lisa Zambetti, Laura Richards, and Jim Clemente of *True Crime Profile* interviewed me on their program. We owe a great deal to many media personalities who kept our story in the public eye.

At the end of the 2017 summer, Abbie and Jean and I were invited to fly to LA to be part of a panel called "The Women of *The Keepers*," hosted by a local investigative reporter. We would be answering questions for an audience made up of those responsible for voting on the docuseries category for the Emmy Awards. Because *The Keepers* does not fit into the same categories as the other Emmy Awards, their votes would be revealed at a smaller non-TV ceremony later.

By this time, Abbie was becoming less comfortable being in the spotlight. She also has a family with grandkids and was more content with research and spending time with them. Abbie's forte became following the status of different states regarding the statutes of limitations on abuse. She also advocates publicly for those laws to change. Abbie Schaub has also been instrumental in investigating the details of Joseph Maskell's time in Ireland. The Irish government has not been able to provide much data due to the privacy issues of the survivors of abuse there.

Returning to Maryland, we met with the family and friends of Sister Cathy. We were all invited to a celebration of Cathy's life in honor of her seventy-fifth birthday. These events were highlights in my journey, reaffirming for all of us that we were doing the right thing for the right reason. Cathy's family is precious, and I have treasured my interactions with them.

16

Empathy, Compassion, Revenge, and Lies

The outward Gemma is not always a reflection of what I am feeling. I did not have empathy for those who were abused by adults because I have never been abused. I could not feel what people and families were feeling, not even my own family, who reacted very differently than I expected to *The Keepers*. For the most part, my younger sister, Maria, and her family knew about the investigation I was undertaking with my Keough colleagues. Maria and her husband, George, had met the filmmakers. They were supportive, but I think they still fear for my safety. My nieces, Chelsea, Gina, and Kristin, are also supportive, and probably more curious than anything. I know they and their young friends think I am a very cool aunt—a badass, fearless warrior.

My older sister, Toni, had been experiencing some health issues during the making of the program. I admit that I poorly chose to tell her what I was doing at the time when she was recuperating from a knee replacement and was on pain medication in the hospital. I remember her saying, "Oh really?" before going back to sleep. Since then, I can see that she "Likes" my comments about the case and the survivors. Recently, Toni asked me how to listen to the podcast I cohost, *Foul Play*. That meant a great deal to me. I wanted my family to understand how critical this story and my advocacy were.

My brother, Jim, had been a student at Cardinal Gibbons High School, the boys' school adjacent to Keough. I had heard about Maskell interacting with some abuser priests there, but my brother is six years younger than I am, so the abuse was never something about which he was aware. When I told Jim about my involvement in *The Keepers*, and that I and many others were going to tell the story in a docuseries, he merely said, "Okay." Then he asked me why I was involved. I reassured him that I had not been a target of abuse, but that many of my friends had been. I explained that because Cathy was such a role model for me, I was driven to find answers and help those affected.

Not having been abused, I feel that I have some emotional distance from the trauma the survivors experience every day. Because of that, I believe I am more able to help however I can. I care very deeply for those who have been harmed and want very much to assist. Compassion is often more difficult, because it takes work on the part of the giver to learn about the other person's pain and heartache, to find out both emotionally and academically what being abused means. I was determined to know as much as I could so that I would never intentionally judge or trigger or question or be ignorant of what each of my friends was dealing with. I read everything I could on clergy abuse. Also, fiction based on truth, nonfiction studies, and documents and timelines. There are numerous documentary productions that cover different aspects of the problem and its ripple effects.

I was so angry for survivors. I wanted to take my voice and new-found notoriety and get back at the church and the clergy and the cops and anybody else who had done bad things. Where was my own anger coming from? Why was I so defiant? It was time to reexamine my motives and beliefs about truth and justice. When was lying okay if it meant finding the truth?

I continue to discover new things about myself. I have learned that some of my anger is because I was in the high school building the entire duration of Maskell's abuse of students there. I was smart. I was good at solving problems and being resourceful. I mingled with many different groups during my years at Keough, so I was angry with myself too, for not knowing, for not being aware enough to rush to someone's aide. I was never a physical fighter. I think when we were little, Mary Jo and I might have had a hair-pulling episode, which was probably my fault because Mary Jo had beautiful straight waist-length hair. I was probably jealous and wanted to pull it. But if I had ever heard screams or crying, or seen a student disheveled or incoherent, I know I would have done something. I would have gone straight to Sister Cathy or Mademoiselle Nugent, my French teacher, who was really French and could have probably kneed Maskell and friends in the groin without hesitation. Remarkably, Sister Cathy's classroom was across the hall from the chapels and Maskell's office. I know she saw and was worried about what was happening. I think there were many more girls who confided in her; I know it. It's horrifying to think that only a one-inch door separated the rest of us from the hell on the other side.

I am always very present in relationships. I watch and listen and am able to take in a lot of information. I was a very happy smart kid with lots of outside interests and hobbies. I have tried many times to picture myself walking down that hall, passing the chapel, passing his office and turning left to continue on to my lesson in chemistry, biology, art. I have to shake my head to regain my balance just thinking about what was happening every day in there, for years. Losing Cathy was a shock and very difficult. But because of the circumstances, we really did go through the stages of grief, so I know some of my anger comes from that. Revenge results from anger, and it is a very dangerous transition. Is revenge sweet? I know that moms and dads, Cathy's students, family and friends would not have hesitated to hurt Joseph Maskell, the other priests and nuns and brothers and cops and soldiers and thugs and all of those who covered this up. As an army, we would have been able to take them all down. Perhaps it is better that we did not know, although we would definitely have been in good company serving time together. But revenge is not what Cathy would have wanted. Every time I resent someone who is hurting children, telling lies, covering for other adults, bullying survivors, I force myself to ask, "What would Cathy do or say?" And here is the answer I get: "Gemma, calm down. Your anger is righteous, but it can also be destructive. If you are cloudy or too emotional, you cannot help people who need you. Be angry at the situation but use what you know in your heart to preserve your integrity. Think deeply before you act or speak or write. Ask loyal friends for feedback. Write your thoughts. Write, write, write. Saying less is more." Okay, folks, Cathy does not go through this whole speech every time I look to her. Sometimes she might just sort of put her finger to her lips to hush my words. Sometimes, she makes me struggle to get there by myself, and often my Ernie steps up next to her, saying, "Cathy, I got this." But you know, sometimes when there is blatant injustice and pain when innocent children and adults are in chaos, she and he give me permission to cut loose and use my voice, my pen, my appearance to make things happen or stop them from happening. To me, Cathy was never a wimp—never. I have heard her friend Gerry Koob say that if she was being hurt or abducted, she would freeze. I have to disagree. She had a good serving of feistiness. I never saw her afraid. I saw her as the epitome of a strong female: articulate, outspoken, loving, gentle, feminine, but not a wimp. Cathy is driving this bus we are on. Feel free to jump on if the spirit so moves you.

Let's talk about lying. Yep, we all do it. My teenage niece asked me about the scene in *The Keepers* when I am talking to James Scannell, a former police officer who worked on the case back in the day. She asked if I lied to him about being so appreciative of his time and telling him I would buy him a crab cake. I had to tell her that I was not being sincere with him. She saw the look I gave to the camera, and said, "You don't like that guy. If you get to be a PI, are you going to lie to get stuff?" It killed me to say yes. Her response? "Okay. Maybe I'll be a PI too. But like *with* you." Our director Ryan White chose to rephrase my behavior. He told me I need another bumper sticker on my old red Jeep with the caption Will Flirt For Information. I guess he knows me pretty well. But I was not hurting anybody; my white lies are little ones. Right?

Many of the bad guys in this story told (and still tell) lies constantly. The Roman Catholic Church has been exposed for lying about knowledge of clerical abuse for centuries. Since the darn Middle Ages, people! The pedophile clergy live a lie. They are psychopaths who deceive children and their families to satisfy their disgusting urges. They cannot be cured. (The eleven treatment centers in the United States should be turned into prisons. It is the only way to keep children and teens safe.) The Archdiocese of Baltimore and other religious institutions are lying every day about these felons. When the church kicks out a priest, guess what happens? The responsibility for that pedophile is no longer on the church; the onus is on the community and society at large to bring him to justice. The credibly accused clergy are now living among the rest of us as unregistered sex offenders. Many of these individuals are even residing on the church's dime in luxury retirement communities. Where do your parents and grandparents live? On a retirement campus? Do you take your babies and young children to see Grandma and Grandpa? Does a nice priest live down the hall? Do your homework. Go on the internet to bishopsaccountability.org. Who is that priest? Ask where they served. Don't be shy: you are protecting your family.

In a podcast episode with the director of communications for the Archdiocese of Baltimore, Sean Caine, my colleague Shane Waters asked *how*, not *if*, the church keeps track of the defrocked and laicized priests (guess who wrote *that* question?). Caine responded, "We don't. If Home Depot or Lowes fires an employee, they don't keep track of where the person is living." Seriously? I listened with my microphone muted during that interview. I felt that Caine would not agree to do it if I was part of the conversation. But Sean, you need to know that you alienated many Catholics, many survivors and their advocates. You had dogs barking in the background, phones ringing, and said "Um" more times than we could count. You were indeed the most unprofessional of any of the guests we have interviewed on *Foul Play*. If you were trying to send the message that we were not important or an inconvenience to your busy day, it did not work. I do not know how you can look at your own children with what you know. How do you sleep at night?

Lying seems to be the norm for anybody who abuses children, for those who protect the abusers, and for those that benefit from the abuse. Money is exchanged and gained. Politicians and law enforcement personnel do not have to look far to find a prostitute if they have connections with the Catholic Church. The last time I was in a church was at Cathy's birthday celebration. It was a beautiful event with a good and kind priest—a loving tribute from Cathy's family and friends. But I did kind of freak out at the end, when some Keough nuns stood on the altar in their nun habits and raised their hands above us to bless us, nuns who probably knew what had happened at the school. No thanks, I'm good. I'm blessed with my ocean and my sky and my sand and my dog and my friends and their truth. Frankly, the only individuals I truly believe in relation to this whole Catholic hot mess are the survivors of the abuse. Why in the world would they show their faces and tell and write their stories and appear on television and in a movie? And yet, the Archdiocese of Baltimore challenges them as liars, and then offers them a pittance for what they have been through. No wonder survivors struggle coming forward and going public. It is traumatizing all over again.

The fact that the abuse was reported as early as 1967 to the Archdiocese of Baltimore is irrefutable, regardless of what their attorneys claim. We know. We have dates. We have the names of parents, and men and women, who told persons in authority. That those persons did not believe them, or threw those notes in the trash or gleefully destroyed records at Keough is criminal and is not the fault of those who told. It remains the fault of those who were hired to protect these children and teenagers. You know who you are. We know who you are. You need to make this right before your last breath. We know you do not want to lose your pensions, but fifty years ago, you did not help Cathy or Russell or Jean or Teresa or Kathy or Lil or Donna. You did not help all the thousands of kids who subsequently suffered because Maskell and Magnus were able to create a network of prostitution, torture, drug abuse, and mind control. You know you lied.

The Attorney General in Maryland is conducting a criminal investigation into clergy abuse all over Maryland: priests, brothers, nuns, deacons, policemen, high-ranking politicians, thugs, businessmen, teachers. As this book goes to print, it is the hope of all of us involved in uncovering the truth that a grand jury will be convened, resulting in the release of all your names and crimes. We are the truth now. You are not. The whole world agrees with us, except the Roman Catholic Church. The next tsunami will not be surreal; it will be as real as the ocean that ceaselessly proves that we are not in charge. Until that day, which is coming soon, we will not rest. Our courageous survivors and our precious children will be our heroes in this fight. We are not going to go away, or sit down, or shut up.

17

Boundaries

I never understood the importance of boundaries until I had to draw them. In my life and career, I always wanted to be accepted, so I was open to everybody. I learned the hard way that boundaries are necessary and healthy. I care too much about what people think of me. I made a habit of appealing to others and opening myself to harmful people and dead-end relationships just to belong. Disengaging with individuals who are not healthy for me became a disdainful but important task.

I'm a nice person. I am easy-going and enjoy making new acquaintances, colleagues, and friends. I can characterize my relationships by how we communicate. I check my text messages first thing in the morning, which for me might be ten o'clock. Only my family and close friends have my phone number. If there are text messages or voicemail, they are important. Then I check private messages on Facebook Messenger. Those are friends and acquaintances. If folks are sending friend requests, that's also how they reach me. I'm very cautious about friend requests, so don't get mad if I decline!

Every day I get very specific questions from some of you about Sister Cathy's death, or whether Jean has remembered who Brother Bob is. I do not share that kind of information. It's difficult to answer each of you individually, so it's better to post those questions on the public Keepers Facebook pages or on *Foul Play*. Tag me there, and I'll answer if I can.

I look at Facebook notifications next. I read comments right away to see if somebody needs information or has a question. Finally, I answer emails. If I did not give you my email address, please do not ask for it—my accounts have been violated several times. Folks have set up false accounts pretending to be me. Now I have two-part authentication so that I get a notification if someone tries to do that. So, whoever did that in Ontario, North Carolina, and Florida, don't flatter yourselves. Get a job or a hobby. Volunteer at a soup kitchen. You should probably also see a good mental health expert.

There are individuals who were very angry with me after *The Keepers* was released. I drew boundaries with those people, although I feel really sorry for them. A few were friends, mostly acquaintances. I received phone calls during which upset survivors or their families yelled at me. I know this is because when someone is drowning, they sometimes try to take the lifesaver down with them. I have a list of names in my head of those with whom I refuse to communicate. I tried; it did not work. Some abuse survivors had me fooled. They were friendly, appreciated any resources I could provide, but at some point I would hear about how resentful they were of me. That really bothered me at first, but I cannot control what other people think. I am comfortable with who I am, regardless of what I am accused of doing or not doing. I do not answer their phone calls or emails, I do not accept friend requests from them or their buddies. I am happy in my life. Determining how far I will let somebody go with pressuring me is now a practice I enforce.

I have also had to draw some boundaries with some of those close to me. If I do not ask for their opinion, but they feel the need to give it, I probably interrupt. Suggestions are not the same as *you should,* or *you need to,* or *you have to.* Gemma answers to her heart and her head, not to trolls or overbearing acquaintances. I have my internal guidelines and stick by them.

I do not share information about survivors, not even those who have gone public. I will not tell you who is utilizing our Sister Cathy Cesnik Survivors Fund. I will not respond to disrespect. But I will tell you what I think, and I will help you if I can. I won't watch Fox News. I will tell you on my Facebook page that I cannot stand President Forty-five. If you want to argue with me about that right there on my page, don't bother. I'll probably delete your comment. It's my page. Go say it on your page, and I will not argue with you there. If you make fun of my appearance, I will not make fun of yours. Don't manipulate me or lie about me—I will definitely call you out on that. Other than those boundaries, I will love you and trust you and welcome you into my home. We will be able to tell if we click or not within a few hours. Uh, I take that back . . . make it a few weeks. I know I scare some guys, but that is likely my own insecurity. I do not like my vulnerability to show. If you get all that and still think I'd be fun as a friend, well that would be cool. Let's do it.

Snowday Blues

Snowing all day,
Gun-metal skies,
That really harsh cold, giving me headaches.
A hollow empty world,
Industrial hues of gray and ash,
Chilly on my couch even under a throw.
Darn cold air sneaking up my back,
Wanting to turn on a lamp,
But wanting not to move.
Silence but for the clicking of heat on and off, 68 degrees,
A shovel rumbles,
Even my red rug looks dull,
Cozy is sometimes hard to be.

18

Alerts, Alarms, Away, Afraid

I beep a lot. Being involved in a murder investigation, filming a documentary, and the resultant effects made it necessary for me to adjust my beeps. As a diabetic, I am used to making short-term changes to my diet, exercise, insulin pump, and all the apps on my phone and hand-held devices that help keep me alive. But now I was dealing with extended periods of time that belonged to other people and institutions. This was scary for me and always demanded that I plan ahead.

Air travel, radio, TV, and newspaper interviews and podcasts forced me to intentionally make accommodations for travel, time changes, unexpected food choices, embarrassing noises and lots of hugging. Usually alone, this was stressful. Sometimes I had to ask for help. Gemma does not like to be vulnerable, and Gemma most definitely does not like to ask for help. My family and close friends are always aware of my health issues, although I really hate feeling needy or singled out. And having "celiac sprue," a disease that means I cannot eat wheat, barley, malt, or rye, means having to ask a million times what is safe for me to eat. Fortunately, in the seventeen years since my diagnosis, life has become much easier for celiac patients. Most restaurants understand and accommodate me, although I still hate asking. But I got this: You do not need to ask for me or ask me if what I am eating is okay. I'll tell you. If you invite me to your home, I'll tell you before I accept.

As soon as filming started, I had to show our filmmakers where all my equipment was located on my body and how it worked. Our cameraman, John Benam, who has become a close friend, always had to make sure my technology was not going to get in the way of his. I wear a tubeless insulin pump called an Insulet Omnipod. It adheres to my skin with a sticky surface and has to be changed and refilled with insulin every three days. I also wear a Dexcom Continuous Glucose Monitor, which tells me via a phone app, what my blood sugar is constantly. The CGM is smaller than my pump but worn in the same manner and changed once a week. All this equipment has settings. Settings with various alerts; alerts for too high, too low, time to change or refill, time to calibrate. I could set some alarms to vibrate instead of beep, but did not always remember. We had a few retakes because I make noise.

Traveling alone from Baltimore to Los Angeles, I had a problem with TSA in my own airport. Stepping up to the counter, I clearly said, "I'm wearing an insulin pump and CGM." TSA agents, I assumed, were trained in this process. As I stepped into the X-ray booth, the agent on the other side told me to get out for a pat down. I wear my equipment interstitially, meaning that each is attached on or near my waist, hips, or rear end. As the female agent attempted to pat me down over my clothing, I physically protected my middle and told her not to touch me there. She said, "It's through your clothing." I responded with determination, "My point exactly. You are going to dislodge my diabetic equipment." Considered uncooperative, a very big dude approached and told me to get out of line and come to the side of the security desk. He made me open my purse and carry-on. Lady agent looked smug. What ensued was a science lesson by me for them about what is what and why I am wearing it all. I had to pull up my shirt so the agents could see that I was not a terrorist. They were harsh, and I got weepy. When I finally got through the security area, I collapsed on a bench, now with low blood sugar and crying. A supervisor followed me to my gate. Now what? I turned to confront him and stood my ground. To my surprise, he apologized for the agents. I told him they needed a come-to-Jesus meeting and a new attitude. He agreed.

For some reason, my name was flagged on the return trip. I was directed to a lane where I did not have to open anything, take off footwear or answer questions. Like a fool, I took off my shoes and put all my jewelry right on the belt because there were no baskets. The rich man behind me laughed and gently told me that I was in the preferred lane and did not have to do any of that. I guess that supervisor wanted my trip home to go well. Thank you, sir.

I have to travel with food. Food for low blood sugar, food for skipped meals, substitutes for food that is not gluten-free. I've come up with some brilliant strategies. KIND bars go anywhere and are good for anything. Juice boxes are tiny and travel well. Wait till you get through security before you buy the good stuff, though, like fruit and sodas. Orange slice candies are cheap, a dollar a bag—two of those bad boys are perfect for low blood sugar. I order a special meal if I am on long flights, but if I am traveling overnight, I do not order a gluten-free meal. I order a fruit plate. Eat some, save some.

No overeating or feeling sick in the middle of the night. Because my CGM tells me what my sugar is and my pump delivers my insulin, I no longer have to climb over people to go to the bathroom on a plane to take insulin injections. I've got this down to an easy system, but I still must be a good planner and calculate well ahead. Whenever I meet new people, I still am nervous that I am going to knock my equipment off or make either you or me uncomfortable. The last boyfriend used to say, "Where's Waldo?" to determine where my equipment was attached to me. *Where's Waldo?* is a book in which the reader has to find a little guy in a big crowd. That's a good line, and you have my permission to use it when we meet.

19

Tribal Dance

It's hard for me to comprehend that so many people in the world now know who I am. This has become both a joy and a curse. The tribe, as my younger sister has christened us, is made up of old new friends, new friends (young and old), people who picked on me and now think I am cool, and significant forever friends who have joined me in this mission. We honor one another, we move in safe circles; I am protected and loved. We cut loose, we work hard, we learn about each other's goals and challenges. The tribe is my diverse reality; some have let me down, but most have held me up. This chapter is about them.

Jean Hargadon Wehner (Jane Doe). The first time I met Jean was at the Double-T Diner on the corner of Route 40 and Rolling Road in Catonsville, Maryland. She had committed to the docuseries, as had Abbie and I, but we had yet to meet. When she arrived, all I saw was a smiling face of freckles and her beautiful red hair. Jean gave us big hugs and we sat down, she on one side of a booth, Abbie and me on the other. We knew Jean was vetting us. She told us that, when she heard about us picking up the reins on Cathy's murder and the surrounding abuse, she was careful. She said others had shown interest, but nobody hung around. She wanted to make sure we were the real deal and could be trusted. Jean is a smart lady. She told us up front that she had only an hour, as she had another commitment that afternoon. It was enough for me to know that this woman had spirit and a warm, but cautious demeanor.

To me, Jean is the hinge of *The Keepers*. Through her experience, she is the connection between Cathy's death and the abuse at Keough. I value her friendship. I find Jean ethereal, and she reminds me very much of Cathy Cesnik: intelligent, diplomatic, often private but loves to talk, and has a great big wonderful laugh. Jean has been through horrific things, so horrific that she repressed many of the most difficult. Because her memories are hers, I do not pry or ask her questions unless she offers information. I keep her confidences. Jean may hold the answers to many mysteries, but that is her business. I am blessed to be in her circle of friends, and I would defend and protect her to the end.

Teresa Lancaster (Jane Roe). I heard about Teresa Harris from a woman at Keough, Mary Spence, who asked me if I had ever talked to her. Mary thought perhaps Teresa had been harmed by Maskell at Keough. I also learned that both Mary and Teresa had been a year behind me at both Saint William's and Keough. Teresa's brother, Mark, had been in my class. Her older brother, Joe, had been my chemistry teacher at Keough. There are no coincidences. Teresa introduced herself to all of us on the AKHS Survivors page. Many of her friends were stunned, but all of us welcomed her courageous move with love and support. An almost audible cheer went up from those of us who were online that night. As more women did the same, the ranks of supporters grew, and stories of pain and abuse were shared.

I first met Teresa when she and her husband, Randy, came to my home for a meeting of survivors, friends and grassroots investigators where she bravely but bluntly told her story. She did not hold back. And, believing her, we all committed to helping her and others however we could. Teresa and I have had our ups and downs. Soon after *The Keepers* was released, she and I were given inaccurate and hurtful information about each other. There was a lot of misunderstanding following the release from different factions. It took us awhile, but Teresa and I have worked our way back to each other. I trust her, and I respect and like her. I admire her outspoken manner about advocacy for survivors. Teresa, like me, is a handful. But we get each other.

Donna Vondenbosch, you will remember from *The Keepers*, is a sweet lady with a very strong Baltimore accent. Though seeming very shy, she is a dynamo: smart, determined and very, very funny. I met Donna for the first time at a get-together at Teresa's home in the fall of 2017. We had been messaging each other, slowly and cautiously at first. Because Donna was given post-hypnotic suggestions by Joseph Maskell never to talk about what happened to her, her written communication was sometimes stilted and unclear. As our friendship has grown, Donna's recovery has been remarkable. Although Donna has had a stroke and a heart attack, she is tough and stubborn. She, like Teresa, did not trust me because of others' comments. Now we are the Three Musketeers. Donna is brilliant. A certified nurse practitioner, she cares about the mental and physical health of abuse survivors; their welfare is a priority. Donna also has a great sense of humor, and we crack each other up, even in text messages. If you have not seen Donna twirl her batons on her Facebook page, you are missing a real treat. She remains one of my forever friends.

Kathy Hobeck was in my class at Keough. None of us knew that she was also among those being abused by Joseph Maskell. But she did tell Cathy. Sister Cathy helped her avoid many calls to his office. Cathy would tell him via the speaker in the ceiling of the classroom that Kathy Hobeck was busy and not available. Kathy visited Sister Cathy one more time the week before she disappeared. Kathy and I have also become forever friends. She requested that I accompany her when she went to her mediation settlement, which was an honor for me. I got a firsthand look at the lack of interest on the part of her attorney and heard the scripted and very insincere conversation at the table. Because her attorney did not expect to see me there, he reacted with childish condescension. He took me aside and said he had heard I was telling people he was in bed with the Archdiocese. I had not, but the comment itself was so unprofessional, I dreaded for Kathy what was to come. When my presence there was questioned by her attorney, who said it was highly unusual, Kathy insisted I was "her person" for the day. I sat next to her, got her a soda and tissues, held her hand. Her own attorney at one point said, "You might as well take it. They won't give you more." Kathy and I had lunch together. I broke the tension with my silliness and imitations of "persons in authority." We laughed all the way home. She is my buddy. What a gal!

Lil Knipp was Maskell's student secretary at Keough. In *The Keepers*, she talked about how he manipulated her with drugs. Lil had the honor of hitting Maskell in the face when he tried to kiss her on the last day of her senior year at Keough. Lil and her husband, George, are two of the easiest people to be around. When they visited me in Ocean City, I was running out the door to take Teddy to the vet with a bloody foot. When I returned several hours later, they were dancing and singing in the kitchen with cocktails and dinner cooking on the stove. We all three share a love of music and art. Once when Lil was here, we spent the day painting and drawing and singing Beatles songs.

Ryan White is the director of *The Keepers*. The first time I met Ryan was in a Home Depot parking lot, where we met to take a ride around the area, stopping at places where significant events happened. I thought he was adorable; I wanted to adopt him immediately. I told Ryan the first time we talked that he was going to have to tell me when to back off or if my opinion was not needed. I explained that I am often too present in relationships and that in my career teaching kids, parents and other educators, that I was used to being in charge. He nodded, but I had to really submerge my bigger-than-life personality many times during our journey. I do not always take direction and after all he was the director. There was a time after *The Keepers* was released that I disappointed Ryan. I had learned that an attorney was using volunteers to get more mediation clients. This is called ambulance-chasing, and it is not legal. The volunteers were told they were working for me, but in reality, they were not. Each volunteer had to sign a Non-Disclosure Agreement under the title of *The Keepers* research team. Because I thought that was clearly a copyright violation, with my name unknowingly connected to it, I wrote to Ryan and Netflix to share what was happening. He responded that sharing this information with the whole Netflix staff was inappropriate and unnecessary. Little did I know that I had just caused a major upheaval at the network and with Ryan. I thought I was helping. I was not. I felt terrible. I felt like I had let God down. Ryan may not have known this, but his wonderful Aunt Kathy helped me work through my apology. I think Ryan still loves me. At least he acts like we are okay. Ryan, pretend we are okay even if we are not, because if you don't, I will beat my head against my pillow until I pass out.

Jessica Lawson Hargrave, our producer, has been Ryan's best friend since childhood. They have been working together as filmmakers all their lives. Jess was the producer for *The Keepers*, but could also film, direct, schedule, make us feel comfortable, mike us, care about us and be my friend. Jess got married during the filming of *The Keepers*. She and her photographer husband, Austin Hargrave, had a beautiful baby girl right after *The Keepers* was released. I miss our conversations. Jessica could be my daughter, but we laughed a lot talking about my failed romances, poor singing voice, and efforts to tell everybody what to do. Once when Jess and I were to pick up food for everybody who was waiting at Abbie's house, we got lost because we were talking too much. Arriving an hour late, our friends were chewing on their wine glasses.

John Benam was the director of photography for *The Keepers*. John and his family have become lifelong friends. After *The Keepers* was released, he invited me to a Keepers discussion group. Nobody knew I would be participating. From the second floor of his home in Baltimore, John contacted me via Skype at home. Once we were connected, he carried me on his laptop down the steps and asked if anybody minded another guest. That was one of the most fun and meaningful events for me that summer. John and Angela Benam and their kids are always welcome in my home. We get together as often as possible. They stick by me. John has gone to bat for me when others are critical of my actions. That's what real friends do.

Abbie Fitzgerald Schaub is one of the smartest people I have ever met. Although we did most of our work online from our own homes, we were able to merge my in-person contacts with her internet and library research. Abbie, who is very left-brained, and me, extremely right-brained, did not process information in the same way, but we were effective as a team. We were able to take our separate findings and put pieces of the puzzle together well. I relied on Abbie for documents, timelines and statistics, while I was able to put names and faces and survivors' stories together. Though we have gone our separate ways, Abbie remains a force to be reckoned with in her work to have the statute of limitations in Maryland eliminated and to track the statistics of abuser priests exposed in Maryland and other states.

Marilyn Cesnik Radakovic is Cathy's sister. You saw our first meeting by phone in *The Keepers*. She and her husband, Bob, are lovely people with a wonderful family. Marilyn and I connected like sisters. She reminds me very much of Sister Cathy. Cathy's siblings did not know about the mystery surrounding Cathy's death and the abuse at Keough. Her mother, Ann, had been keeping track of all the newspaper clippings but, until Ann's death, the rest of the family was protected from the horrors we all now know about. I know this has been a difficult transition for all the Cesnik/Radakovic family members. Their willingness to participate in *The Keepers* and to be known around the world are testaments to their love for Cathy. Their determination to bring justice for her and all those who were harmed and deceived by the abusers and the Catholic Church speaks volumes about this amazing family. Respecting the privacy of Cathy's family is essential; their lives were changed by the discovery of what happened to her fifty years ago.

Marguerite "Pat" Gilner has an essential role in this story. Because she attended the novitiate with Cathy and Russ, she was an important part of both their lives. It was Pat who moved in with Russell after Cathy disappeared. You met Pat in *The Keepers*, sitting in her lovely apartment amid her artwork and white décor. As a nun, Pat was an art teacher; now she continues to share that gift with many still. It was Pat who planned Cathy's birthday celebration in Maryland with Cathy's family. She is one of the most giving, loving women I have ever met. Fun, funny, talented and brilliant, her manner is also very much like Cathy's.

Christine Centofanti was a year ahead of me at Keough. You met Chris in *The Keepers* because she was close friends with Russell after Cathy's death. Chris was instrumental as the real estate agent for Russ and her family when they moved away from Baltimore County. I confide in Chris when I am confused, when I have decisions to make and need a sounding board. Always busy, but never too busy to listen. Chris was also fortunate to have visited Cathy and Russ in the weeks before Cathy's death, to share the news of her engagement to her sweet husband, Vince. Chris and I are united in believing that Russell Phillips was in a very difficult position when Cathy was murdered. She lost her best friend less than twenty-four hours after likely being threatened by those responsible for her murder. Russell died a few days after Pat informed her of Masksell's death. Her husband, John, requested privacy in light of the events in *The Keepers*. The tribe respects and honors his wish.

Michele Stanton is my "Sister Cathy Survivors' Fund" partner and hippie buddy. Her perspective on the abuse and murder of Cathy is unique because she met Cathy and Russ at their apartment before she even attended Keough. Michele lived in the neighborhood and visited the nuns with her older friends. She had no idea they were nuns. Michele was abused by Edgar Davidson and James Scannell when she was a young teenager; she was also targeted by Neil Magnus and Joseph Maskell when she entered Keough. Michelle had no idea how these three events were connected until she saw *The Keepers*. Michele's work as a psychotherapist enables her to understand her own trauma and that of other survivors. As of this writing, Michele and her husband Jon are completing the paperwork necessary to make the Sister Catherine Cesnik Survivor's Fund a nonprofit organization. The fund provides financial assistance towards therapy for survivors of clergy abuse.

Charles Franz was my neighbor during the filming of *The Keepers*. Halfway through the journey, a mutual friend told me that she knew he and his wife were both survivors of abuse by Maskell. I had no idea that the quiet, subdued guy who walked his little dog and lived across the lawn was part of this story. Our friend told me he wanted to talk to me about mediation and the film. Taking Teddy across the yard, Charles was sitting on his steps like he was waiting for us. His story was credible and incredibly poignant. His mom and the mother of another boy went downtown in 1967 to the offices of the Archbishop of Baltimore to report that their sons were being drugged and abused at St. Clement's by none other than Joseph Maskell. Charles is the real deal. His story broke our hearts. When the Doe/Roe case hit the news in 1993, the archdiocese reached out to Charles, supposedly to offer him support and counseling. Why? What did he need counseling for? He knew nothing about the Doe/Roe case. Reverend Malooly and two archdiocesan attorneys scheduled a meeting with Charles at his office. Charles shared with us, and the world, that he was offered a boat to keep his mouth shut. What triggered their visit? Think about this: if Charles had been subpoenaed by the prosecuting attorneys in the Doe/Roe case, his story would have corroborated theirs. All Charles asked for was the truth. Fortunately for the archdiocese, the case never went to trial. Following the release of *The Keepers*, the Catholic Church has called Charles a liar. But Charles is a hero, and the church knows it.

Mary Ann Driscoll is a name most of you may not recognize. Mary Ann is probably the oldest of the Maskell survivors that we know about. She was thirteen and played the organ at St. Clement, the first parish where Maskell was assistant pastor. Mary Ann did not attend Keough but was subjected to horrific abuse by Maskell for many years in the rectory and church. We have become dear friends and trust each other implicitly. When she comes to visit me at the beach, Mary Ann insists on cooking, cleaning, and walking Teddy. It's like having another sister.

Sharon Bush attended Keough a year ahead of me. You met Sharon if you listened to the *Foul Play* podcast interview she did with Shane Waters and me. She was very close friends with Russell Phillips. She was able to help complete the gaps in the timeline of the day Cathy disappeared and the events of the day after. It is through Sharon, that we learned that Russell knew of the abuse at Keough. But it is because of Sharon that I have gained a very good friend. Sharon is honest, giving and nonjudgmental. We have both dealt with caring for loved ones with serious health issues; we both understand what is important in life and what is trivial.

My family has supported me all my life. I have three siblings, Toni, Maria, and Jim; three nieces, Gina, Kristin, and Chelsea; a great-niece, Charlotte; and two great-nephews, Drew and Wyeth. We spent more time together when my mom was living, but we are all there for each other when needed. My younger sister went to Keough, three years behind me. Several of her classmates are also survivors of abuse. Maria and I were not abused. I am excited for my family to relive childhoods through my memories here. And I want them to know that I appreciate and value their love. I know they worry about me, but I always seem to get through challenges, if not unscathed, at least alive. You can say it with me now, "I keep on keeping on!"

My friends, old and new make my life full. They play a significant role in this tribe. My teacher friends spent the weekend with me when *The Keepers* aired. Mary Sliwinski, Bev Hibschman, and Marian Stewart kept me busy and let me be real. We all cried, laughed at my weird hair, and ate junk food while we binged the series. I will love them forever for never judging me and always accepting my sometimes-unconventional ideas.

Another childhood friend, *Jackie Bierman*, is a person who got me interested in Cathy's story many years ago. (If you recall, she was the friend who suggested we take that upside-down pizza to visit the Carriage House Apartments in the summer of 1969.) Jackie sent me newspaper clippings over the years, anytime there was new attention on the case, and she and I have continued to stay close, although because of her former position as a police officer, she chose not to be filmed in *The Keepers*. No secret, just a personal choice.

Other friends have come into my life more recently. The two Patties were at Keough in my sister's class and each reached out to me separately because they have vacation homes here at the beach. *Patty Bent* has been invaluable finding and organizing internet data. *Patty Faust* comes to my aid with rides, tickets to music events, and invitations to eat crabs. But the most important thing about these two ladies is that we have formed a trio in which we can say anything, laugh our heads off, listen to each other's worries and challenges without worrying about confidentiality. Patty Faust is a relatively new widow, while Patty Bent is disabled from a surgical procedure gone wrong, and you know what a hot mess I am. We fill in the blanks for each other, intuitively knowing who needs what and when.

Many other *Keough alumnae* have reentered my life and each other's. Those from my own class, 1970, I have seen at reunions. But now, because some of our classmates have shared that they are survivors of abuse at the hands of Maskell and others, we all have a very special bond. I value their opinions and treasure their support. Women from every Keough graduating class from 1969 through 2017 have joined the AKHS Survivors page on Facebook. At last count, over 800 women have joined, either to tell their stories or to offer support and advocacy. Those who attended during the Maskell years, 1967 through 1975, often discuss what happened and how most of us were unaware of the monsters among us.

My students. Many of my former students have found me and jumped into this adventure with me. They are mostly in their forties and fifties. Some are grandparents, which is very hard for me to believe. They support me and this mission. They remind me of what I taught them, that nobody deserves to be bullied, and that integrity and intelligence are partners with humor and fun. I loved teaching those kids, and now, as fine adults, they have come into my life again. They and their parents have visited me, offered to help me, called to say hey, and sent pictures of our days together at Magnolia, Jarrettsville, or Abingdon Elementary schools. If I taught you, please get in touch via Facebook. You were my life for many happy years.

Sisters, as in nuns, have also jumped into this arena with me. I have three sister friends who get me and agree with us that the Church needs to do some major renovations. *Sister Rose Pacatte* is a movie reviewer who lives in Los Angeles. She interviewed me when *The Keepers* was released and later did a podcast with Shane and me about how Cathy and Russ were able to leave the convent. She did a good job explaining that, although it is still confusing to me. My takeaway was that nuns are not all sisters or the other way around. She has also given me encouragement and feedback while I have been writing this book. We plan to meet when I am in Los Angeles.

Sister Agnes is very much a rebel, though I don't want to get her kicked out of her order by saying too much. She told me her pastor said she had to get rid of her Facebook account. I think she did for like a minute; now she is back again.

Sister Patricia has lived in South America and has seen clergy abuse rampant in some of those countries. She keeps me posted on happenings there and always gives me good feedback on my activities here.

Bob Erlandson is everybody's "hon." He covered the story of the Doe/Roe trial with his writing partner, Joe Nawroski. Bob is my idol because he is an incredibly gifted writer but is also a staunch Democrat and says it like it is. He loves dogs, adding to his charm. Bob was thoughtful and sage in *The Keepers* and can't figure out Sister Russell either. Bob met Ernest Hemingway a long time ago. I have a photo of them together. Who met Hemingway? Bob did.

Tom Nugent is one of the founding fathers of this tribe. He and I do not always agree, but we respect each other's opinions and honor each other's work. I owe Tom a great deal of thanks; he originally engaged with me about Cathy, and we worked together to bring renewed attention to the investigation into her murder and the abuse at Keough. Recently Tom told me he needed to have a difficult conversation with me. He shared that an individual we both knew had spread some damaging rumors about me, and he needed to know if they were true. I appreciate that Tom stepped up to ask me flat out. What was being said surprised me, and I reassured Tom that none of the story was true. Tom was gracious and relieved. We are in a good place.

Greg Ellison did the first print interview with me just before *The Keepers* was released. News outlets were allowed to see some but not all the episodes in order to be able to do interviews with us ahead of time. Netflix was receptive to Greg's request because he was local, and I lived in the town where he worked as a news reporter for *Ocean City Today*. (In case you did not know before, now you know where I live.) I met Greg in March 2017, walking down the front street with Teddy. Nobody else was on the street. He stopped to greet my dog. Very cute but way too young for me, I still used my go-to line, "I'm not hitting on you, but I have a story you might want to cover." Now we are besties. Greg did me the honor of writing several more articles about the series and the Survivors Fund. He also took the photographs for this book. Greg Ellison is very good guy. Another forever friend.

Shane Waters, as you know, allows me to cohost his podcast, *Foul Play*. We have become great colleagues and friends. He and his girl-friend, *Alecia Rapp* have been guests in my beach home. We traveled to Baltimore to visit many of the people involved in this story and the places where events happened. Shane and I are resolute in our commitment to keep on looking for answers. Although he could be my grandson, Shane is a true buddy. I trust him completely, and I think he feels the same. Shane's friend, *Wendy Cee*, is a moderator on the podcast. Wendy is a wild and crazy lady from the United Kingdom. She keeps me sane and knows what to say or not say, and when. Wendy has pink and purple hair right now. I can't wait to meet her.

Grae Huddleston is now one of my dearest tribal friends. He often posted on *The Keepers* Facebook page about the series and asked lots of intriguing questions. I thought his name was Grace and that he was a female, but when I friended him, I found out I was reading the name incorrectly. One night, Grae FaceTimed me to see if it was really me who had friended him. "Hi. Yes, it is really me." Since that day almost a year ago, we talk every day. He is hilarious, smart and knows more about *The Keepers* than I do. One time, he asked if he could read some questions. Of course, I agreed. He had questions about every episode. Grae also has a sixth sense. I am not into psychic stuff, but he gets images in his head and dreams that are often accurate. I have a list in my phone called "Grae's Premonitions." We are still waiting for most of them to happen. When he asked if the word "bluejay" meant anything, I remembered that one of the MKUltra (mind control) projects was called "Bluebird." And he did come close with the name "Officer Spanky" (I had heard about a bad cop named Sharkey). However, we are still waiting for a ballerina and a heavy silver box to show up. You never know.

Grae could be my son, not my boyfriend. He is flamboyantly gay and keeps me laughing. He helps me pick outfits from my closet and gives me fashion tips. Grae works at a very high-end restaurant in Palm Springs, California. I want him to get Goldie Hawn and Kurt Russell to say my name out loud the next time they come in. Grae and I are going to see Adam Lambert in concert at some casino there. Christmas in California gives me the opportunity to see my Tripod Media friends as well.

There are so many other wonderful people who deserve to be acknowledged here for their advocacy, friendship and assistance. They are all very special members of *The Keepers* tribe.

So, everybody put on your red shoes and let's dance:

Makowske family and friends	John and Mary Ellen Dunnigan	Diana and Bobby Jr. Beales
Sharon and Pete Roe	Georgia Pence	Debbie Fisher
Anne Roberts	Anjili Babbar	Anne Meyers Copeland
Morsequale Family	Sam Ketterman	Bruce Weal
Steffany Ann Topping	Erin Labor	The Bayside Skillet Family
Christian Schaffer	Bob Thomas	Kristin Dilley
Matt Mazur	Mark Harrison	White/McCabe Family
Christine DuFrane	Cindy Lovell	Gloria Larkin
Anne Farrell	Cathy Farrell	Dan Cuddy
Nancy Sjoljinski	Dan Smith	Debbi Hamill Persinger
Mary Jean Bohager	Margaret and Carl Apfelbach	Philis and Ben Scarfii
Charissa Pretto-Huie	Bonner family	Sandy Paws Pet Store
Pat Bennett	Leslie Schell	Stephanie McVey
Sam McCartney-Ditka	Tracy Myers	Joyce Foley
Kate Collins	Sandy Bishop Swift	Rosemarie Law
Gary Childs	Robin Teal	Richard Wolf

Jack Kinsella	JRC Jewelry	Mary and David Smith
Laura Richards	Jim Clemente	Lisa Zambetti
Jeanne Kushner	Jim Cabezes	Ramsey Flynn
Laura Bassett	Amy and Mike Ranahan	Kim Bonham
Barbara Sheridan	Kendall Skirven	Kevin Turowsky
Valarie Dalfonzo	Anne Garson McGuire	Mary Garson
Vicki Ruth Marshall	Janice Lent	Susan Ensor
Susan Quirk	Lynn Schirmer	Erin Lokey
Juliana Bertaldi	Mary Spence	Robert Heath (my bodyguard)
Norton Family	Scott Aversano	Nolan Family
Stefan Freed	Tom Drumm	Sheila Mahoney
John Barnold	Kevin Palmer	Malecki Family

I wrote this a few days before *The Keepers* was released.
I reread it often.
It brings me back to where I am and why.

REALIZATIONS

So, I am sitting in the dark on my swing with my dog, listening to the waves crashing on our beach.

Like no one else is alive.

And the world tonight feels so big. And Nature is in charge. We are tiny specks.

But then I think of each of you, my old friends and my family, my new friends—yes, the tribe.

Our tiny specks are together making winds and waves of voices; some loud and strong, some soft and sweet, some soothe, some excite, some tell me we're okay.

And then I know our energy feeds off our passion for living and caring and knowing the right thing to do.

And we Keepers keep on doing it, even when we get scared.

There's always another soul or friend to hold hands with.

We don't ever have to be afraid because we face ugly things as one, and if one of us can't punch the lights out of the damn devil, someone else can spit in his eyes and kick his butt.

And we can change this world for kids and each other.

I think it has begun.

20

Who Killed Sister Cathy? (Reprise)

Some of you have peeked ahead at this last chapter. I probably would have done the same thing. This is where I am going to tell you what I think happened to Sister Catherine Cesnik. Please remember that this is speculation, so consider this a disclaimer. I do not want to debate or fight or be sued or get killed. If I get threats, I will call the police and my bodyguard Robert, so please do not do that.

My theory is partly based on what I have learned from those who knew her, as well as those who did not but who knew the suspects under consideration. Unless there is a confession, an eyewitness, or a DNA match, I will likely never know if my theory is even close. All of it is circumstantial, but to me, my ideas make sense. I probably do know more than most of you because I have connections with the police, some private investigators, and media outlets. I am a relentless pest. I do not hesitate to ask questions, figuring the worst that can happen is that somebody tells me to go away. You are welcome to agree or disagree with me; that is your business. I am just putting this out there as one possible answer to who killed Cathy Cesnik.

On the evening of Thursday, November 6, 1969, Cathy and Russell were visited by a Keough student and her boyfriend. The young woman had already shared with the nuns that she had been abused by Reverend Joseph Maskell, the chaplain at Archbishop Keough High School. Very shortly after their arrival at the Carriage House Apartments, Russell offered refreshments to the teenagers and rose to get those. The door to the apartment opened. Two priests from Keough, Joseph Maskell, and Neil Magnus entered without knocking. Perhaps they had seen the teens arrive. People have told me that it was not unusual to see Maskell in this neighborhood. One person remembered him sitting on the front steps of a house up the street talking to some kids.

We know from *The Keepers* that Maskell had already confronted Jean Hargadon (Jane Doe) when she returned to school in September, angry that she had confided in Cathy. He likely was watching the other girls who had been assaulted. I asked that woman about the demeanor of the priests that evening. Her response was that Maskell looked angry and Magnus looked dumb. Cathy quickly ushered the young people out of the apartment. Nobody knows what happened in the apartment after that on Thursday evening. My guess is that the priests threatened the nuns not to report or discuss anything about what they knew was going on. My gut also tells me that Cathy had already reported Maskell to her superiors. A few years ago, a woman shared with me that an employee of the archdiocese revealed witnessing a religious sister in authority destroying paper records a year after Cathy's death. I have begged this person to share this information with the police but have no way of knowing if this has happened because the Cesnik cold-case officers are not permitted to share anything publicly. (Many of you ask me about that and some do not believe it. If I was told significant information or saw confidential files, and someone was arrested and charged with Cathy's murder, I could be subpoenaed to testify about what I had seen. The case could be thrown out as a mistrial. Just us knowing what is in files can seriously impact the outcome of an investigation. But, believe me, I would tear out my eyelashes and all my teeth to see the files on Cathy's case.)

The next day—Friday, November 7—Cathy went to work at Western High School where she taught English. The nuns shared a car and Russ worked at Rock Glen Junior High School, which is adjacent to the apartments. Russ probably walked to school. I have often wondered if the teachers there were made aware that Edgar Davidson was trolling the neighborhood trying to pick up girls from the school. The anonymous young woman from the night before went to school as well, but to Keough. Cathy and Russ were no longer there. She was alone. She shared with me that on that morning, Maskell called her out of class and told her that if she repeated anything she knew or saw, that he would kill her boyfriend and her family. I truly cannot imagine how she or either of the nuns were able to go to school that day.

We know from Juliana Bertaldi in *The Keepers* that she had an English class with Cathy in the afternoon. Juliana says that Cathy seemed fine and chatted about going shopping for an engagement gift for her sister. We learned from Juliana recently that Cathy invited her to go shopping with her. Juliana lived on the other side of the city and did not have transportation. Cathy would have had to drive a half hour to get Juliana and then return her home. That would be typical of Cathy. Juliana politely refused because she had to get home to get dinner going for her family. To me, this indicates that Cathy did not think anything unexpected was going to happen that evening. She would never intentionally put a student in danger.

Cathy and Russell arrived home from school in the afternoon. Sharon Bush, a former Keough student, was a friend of both but especially close to Russ. Sharon stopped by in the late afternoon; Sharon thinks she was either picking something up or dropping something off. Because the nuns did not have many street clothes, girls and their families often loaned or gave them clothes to wear. Sharon believes she left to go home for dinner at around 5:00 pm. The autopsy report from Medical Examiner Werner Spitz indicates that Cathy had eaten ham and sweet potatoes, which was probably what she had for dinner.

I have learned from the Baltimore City Police Department missing person files on Cathy that she left the apartment at approximately 7:30 pm. Her first stop was the bank to cash her paycheck. The police report and Sharon both indicate that the nuns used the First National Bank, at that time in Catonsville on Frederick Road. This bank is not near the Edmondson Village Shopping Center. Cathy then drove to Edmondson Village. While there, a former Keough student and her mother spoke to Cathy in the parking lot of that shopping center. Cathy would have had to go across the highway to the Hecht Company, which was directly across from the other stores, to buy the bakery goods from Muhley's Bakery. At that time, Muhley's was inside the Hecht store itself. It does not appear that the necklace owned by Debbie Yohn and featured in *The Keepers* was bought by Cathy. The police have ruled it out, proposing that Edgar Davidson was a petty thief and may have stolen the necklace at some point. We have heard from several individuals who have the same necklace in different birthstones. None of those were purchased at the Edmondson Village shopping center. We have also learned that the police questioned a woman who worked in the bridal registry at the Hecht Company. She recalled Cathy asking how to set up a registry. There is no record showing that Cathy did so.

The police report from the Baltimore City police indicates that Cathy's car was seen back at her apartment in her parking space at 8:30 pm. My Keough friend, Mary Spence, drove recently to each of the places Cathy may have gone, timing how long it took to get to each. She and her husband were able to do it in an hour but with very little time to spare, and not knowing how long Cathy was at each location. The city report indicates that an airline stewardess who lived in Cathy's building recognized her car there at 8:30 pm but was not able to tell if anybody was in the car. This is contrary to the original story we heard that the woman saw Cathy in the car.

According to the city police, Cathy's car was seen parked awkwardly at the intersection of North Bend Road and Lantern Court as early as 10:00 pm that night. Several residents on the adjacent courts remember seeing the car there at 10:30, 11:00, and midnight. If this is accurate, whatever happened to Cathy happened quickly. The police officer who responded to the missing person call is documented as taking that report at 1:35 am.

I believe that a now-deceased Baltimore County police officer named Robert Zimmerman may have killed Cathy Cesnik. His name came across my radar early in 2019, when an individual from the St. Clement parish contacted me, sharing that Maskell often did ride-alongs with Zimmerman in Lansdowne, yelling at kids to get off the street corners. The individual told me that Zimmerman was a bully and a jerk, but that certainly does not mean he is a murderer. I spent a lot of time processing this possibility. I found that the Fraternal Order of Police (FOP) had honored Zimmerman as a fallen hero, the article calling him Brother Bob. It had never occurred to me that this was how the FOP referred to each other.

I communicated with many people who knew Zimmerman. I asked several Keough women if they would look at his picture. They agreed. Four of those women recognized him as one of their most violent abusers. Only Jean Wehner will ever be able to identify who Brother Bob is, because Jean is the only person who remembers someone being called that. She shared with the world that someone Maskell referred to as Brother Bob said he killed Cathy with a pipe. All the women who recognized Zimmerman from the photo I sent them reported recognizing him to the criminal investigator Richard Wolf at the attorney general's office. They also reported the information to the detective assigned to sex crimes in Baltimore City and to officer Robin Teal in Baltimore County. (I told you—we're a tribe). I have no idea what the police know about him. I have sent the police everything I was able to find out about this man. And there was a lot to send. Only time will tell if he is ever revealed as the perpetrator.

I also think that Joseph Maskell choreographed Cathy's murder. She was collateral damage because she knew too much. I think she was a whistleblower, and I think that she could have taken down the whole monstrous network. I believe that Edgar Davidson and the Schmidt men were also players in the death of Cathy Cesnik. Their own families reached out to us and to the police with this information. If Maskell circulated in the ring of criminals, there were many who would take money to do his jobs. They could easily have been involved in abducting Cathy, cleaning up the crime scene and disposing of her body.

James Scannell died in November 2016, about ten months after we interviewed him for *The Keepers*. Again, I am speculating, but I think he could also have been involved in the design to kill Cathy. Zimmerman worked under Scannell at the Wilkens district police station in southwestern Baltimore County. I did not trust Scannell the day I met him, and to this day believe he took secrets to his grave.

I never believed that Gerry Koob was involved in Cathy's death. I think they loved each other deeply and would never have hurt each other. I have no idea what Koob knows or does not know about the abuse or what happened to Cathy, but he was not, in my opinion, involved.

Although Joyce and Cathy did not know each other, I believe their murders are connected. Joyce was a parishioner at St. Clement, where Maskell was the assistant pastor. Her family has been told nothing by the FBI, and recently the status of the FOIA request that Abbie filed years ago was changed. The letter received in 2019 indicates that because this is a cold case, the file may never be released to the family. A sister of one of Joyce's friends told me a few years ago that Joyce could not stand Maskell; she thought he was a creep. Her family also heard recently that Joyce told Maskell that if he ever touched her younger sister she would kill him.

Joyce's body was found on the grounds of the Fort Meade army base, so her case was handled by the FBI. Maskell was the chaplain there at the base. At the time, he was likely counseling many soldiers returning from Vietnam with PTSD. It would not have been difficult for Maskell to find and pay an unstable soldier to kill Joyce. I learned that the way she was trussed, with her hands behind her back and her throat slit, is the way American soldiers were trained to kill the Viet Cong. In my gut, I think that because these two women told Maskell "no" and to go to hell or to fuck himself, that they paid a price.

Now, I know what is going to happen next. You are going to tell your friends that "Gemma said . . . " "Gemma knows . . ." But Gemma does not know what happened to Cathy or Joyce or Grace or Pam or Danny or Heather. They are probably all connected because of the network of monsters preying on children at the time in the southwest area of Baltimore County and city. You are welcome to debate the circumstances. If I knew for certain what happened, I would tell you. I am waiting like the rest of the world and their families, but while I am waiting, I am talking to everybody about these young people who met a terrible fate because they were children. I am reading and researching and trying to weasel my way into institutions that don't want me poking my nose in their business. But now if you think you might want to join me in that work, I sure could use your help. The tribe welcomes you to find the truth and change the world for kids.

EPILOGUE

Miles to Go

Teddy and Mommy are walking down our beach. It's October, so we are safe from breaking the leash law. I've been caught twice with him during non-dog months, so I am always cautious. Approaching us is a beautiful Labrador retriever with its person. "Friendly?" I query. "Yep, very," is the response from the owner. "Hey, I know you. Are you Gemma?"

This happens to me several times a week. We chat; they ask about the series and what I am doing now. Our dogs play or bark or make faces at each other. My answer is the same. "I'm still digging. There's more to learn." Eventually, I give the podcast a plug and we agree to Facebook friend each other. I've met so many kind and caring dog owners this way. Without the dog thing, we would likely say "hey" and move on.

The same thing goes down in grocery stores, restaurants, and even on the crowded summer beach. "You look familiar. Have we met?" "Excuse me for interrupting your dinner, but we want to thank you for your work." One lady blew me a kiss walking by an outdoor table where I was eating with friends. Her husband gave me a thumbs up. I consider these overtures a blessing and an opportunity to meet good people in my beach town.

My days begin late. I stay up until 3:00 am looking for new information, watching interrogation strategies on YouTube, reading, shopping, and watching movies on my phone. Teddy is my alarm clock and my priority when I get up the next day. He is on the same schedule, so he usually does not start licking my face until 10:00 or 11:00 am. He sleeps on my bed. Teddy can't quite jump up, so he waits patiently for me to pick him up under his belly with both arms and get him settled in. We tried a set of steps for him to climb to get on the bed, but they don't really fit in my room and he prefers his mom to pick him up. You might recall a video we made trying those steps out. I put a treat on the bed, and he leaps up without touching the steps. But if he gets a treat for going to bed, he will want one for breathing and eating and pooping. No.

With coffee and phone in hand, I spend two hours each day just catching up with texts, messages, Facebook and emails. I check in with my three buddies, Shane, Wendy, and Grae. We have a thread on Messenger that has existed for almost a year. We reassure each other that we are fine or not fine. Shane and I usually discuss our plans for upcoming podcast episodes, which involves a lot of long-distance teamwork. We must contact our guests and send them questions from you or ourselves. Working around our guests' schedules and needs comes next. Explaining how our Zoom meeting will work is essential, for many of our guests are not familiar with recorded interview procedures. Once the episode is recorded, Shane goes to work editing and polishing, then sends it to our guest for additional edits or approval. Recording an interview can take as long as three hours. His task is to eliminate excessive noise, like Teddy barking, and extraneous information. We often use one guest's interview for two or three episodes. Podcaster partner Shane Waters and I have recorded over forty episodes of *Foul Play*. We have had the opportunity to talk to and record individuals who were not able to be participants in *The Keepers*. Because we believe that Joseph Maskell may have been involved in the CIA-funded Project MKUltra (a mind control program), our guests have included experts in that field, therapists who treat MKUltra survivors and MKUltra survivors themselves. Recently we interviewed the hunter whose young son discovered Sister Cathy's body in January of 1970.

On Wednesdays after each episode is released, listeners share their thoughts, opinions and questions. Foul Play Discussion Group on Facebook is unique in that we do not tolerate disrespect, bullying or harassment on that page. Our growing group finds it refreshing but spirited. All opinions are welcome, but bullying is not. I invite you to download the free app called Himalaya so that you can also listen to our podcasts. As of this writing, Shane Waters and I are presently in negotiations with a production company for a possible sequel to *The Keepers*. A different format, different filmmakers, different perspective, but always with the goal of sharing a story of courage and integrity about individuals who are ready to speak up and speak out.

I spend a lot of time communicating with the Keough survivors in my life; we really are a tribe of good friends. Answering messages from folks who want to report abuse or need help finding therapy or an attorney is also an important investment of my time. Our Sister Catherine Cesnik Survivors Fund helps defray the cost of therapy for survivors of sexual abuse; my friend and colleague Michele Stanton and I organize and facilitate that. During August 2019, the fund reached twenty-five thousand dollars, making it eligible for nonprofit status.

I still receive emails from media outlets and other podcasters who would like me to do interviews or make presentations. I accept most of those offers because I believe that our story needs to be in the public eye until we have answers. It is also critical to me that I forward any information I get from you, the public, about the murders or the pedophile ring in which Maskell was enmeshed. Everything I receive goes to the correct law enforcement jurisdiction in Maryland. Cathy Cesnik and Joyce Malecki are among several murders of young people in and around that time, and we and the police think that some of these crimes are connected.

Dealing with online attacks is, unfortunately, part of my life now. Ignoring those who find power in spreading rumors or outright lies about those of us who participated in *The Keepers* is not easy. I have done my share of responding, asking why, and defending myself and our survivors. My emails have been hacked and posted; private messages between me and others have somehow been made public as well. I have had to tighten up my Facebook settings and email accounts. Violation of my privacy feels so invasive. I am learning to spend more time writing, painting, and walking the beach. Not engaging in social media at all has been necessary for my own peace of mind and personal safety. The police in my town are aware of my situation and check on me regularly. Making a cyberbullying police report to them was strange but necessary.

Overall, I truly love my life. Living in a beach town on the Eastern Shore of Maryland, I am never bored or lonely. A part of each day is still spent trying to put the pieces of these interlocking puzzles together. My philosophy is that every day be spent doing something productive, something therapeutic and something fun. My writing and my artwork, my dog and my beach, my people and their stories all fill my world. And of course, CNN. My guilty pleasure is to watch *Dr. Phil* at 4:00 pm. The seriously dysfunctional individuals on that program make the rest of us look like saints.

I am determined to remain active with this mission that has chosen me until I cannot do it anymore. Every day brings some new surprise to keep me keeping on. Some justice for Sister Catherine Cesnik has already been found in the impact her short life has had all over the world. We who champion and advocate for those she touched are now her voice. Her legacy will live on as society changes, the Catholic Church is exposed, and survivors of sexual abuse everywhere are able to find their own voice and speak their truth. I am honored to be, with all of you, a part of that movement. We are changing herstory.

Higher Power

Somewhere

Anywhere

Nowhere

Now here

Science can't explain infinity

Blue explained, rainbow, moon, sun and clouds too

But not sky

Look up

Which is really out

It never ends

For me this is the proof.

Appendix

RESOURCES FOR SURVIVORS OF SEXUAL ABUSE

SNAP (Survivors Network of those Abused by Priests)
Toll free phone: 1-877-SNAP-HEALS (1-877-762-7432)
General information: (314) 776-9277
Website: snapnetwork.org
Includes contact information for local chapters and for the state attorney general offices currently conducting investigations into clergy abuse. Report abuse to your attorney general's office.

RAINN (Rape, Abuse and Incest National Network)
24-hour hotline: 1-800-656-4673
RAINN is a nonprofit and the nation's largest organization dealing with sexual assault.

Childhelp National Child Abuse Hotline
1-800-422-4453

Website: childhelp.org

US nonprofit organization dedicated to the prevention, intervention, and treatment of child abuse.

National Suicide Prevention Lifeline
24-Hour Hotline: 1-800-273-8255

Bishop Accountability
Website: bishopsaccountabilty.org

Educational enterprise documenting the abuse crisis in the Roman Catholic Church.

Includes a US database of clergy credibly accused of sexual abuse by diocese.

Find a therapist
psychologytoday.com

lp.talkspace.com

betterhelp.com

Financial assistance for sexual abuse therapy
Gofundme.com. Search for Sr. Cathy Cesnik Fund for Survivors (provides financial help for survivors of clergy abuse in the Archdiocese of Baltimore. Priority given to those abused by Reverend Joseph Maskell or Reverend Neil Magnus).

MEDIA REFERENCES

The Keepers: Netflix docuseries, May 2017

Foul Play podcast: available on the free app Himalaya. Forty-plus episodes dealing with the murder of Catherine Cesnik and Joyce Malecki, as well as the sexual abuse of children and teens at the hands of pedophiles in the Archdiocese of Baltimore.

Bassett, L. May 14, 2015. "Buried in Baltimore: The Mysterious Murder of a Nun Who Knew Too Much," *The Huffington Post*.

Mandelbaum, P. December 1995. "God Only Knows," *Baltimore Magazine*.

Nugent, T. 2006. "Who killed Sister Cathy?" *The Baltimore City Paper*. Article is now available at whokilledsistercathy.wordpress.com

FILES FROM BALTIMORE CITY POLICE DEPARTMENT MISSING PERSONS REPORT FOR CATHERINE CESNIK

NOTES:

- Text in brackets added by me, Gemma Hoskins.
- These files were obtained under the Maryland Public Information Act and received on September 26, 2019. There were 37 pages, including one duplicate. A few pages were missing.
- The text is reproduced here as written in the original documentation, including spelling and punctuation errors, which does make them tricky to read in places.
- Question mark (?) indicates name copied from handwritten report. Some letters were illegible.
- Any explanations of terminology needed are provided in square brackets set by me.
- Unless otherwise noted all reports have some or all the following info in the header in one form or another: Cesnik, Catherine (A.) / Tel. xxx–xxxx / Complaint No. xxxxxxx / Original Report Date: 8 Nov. 69 / 131 North Bend Rd. / Missing Person / Occurrence: 7 Nov. 1969 – 7:30 PM / Post: 826

Reporting officer(s) supervisor approving text, DJS. Comments 08-Nov-69 1:35 am. Robert H. Becker ?) 2976 SW Sgt. J.T. Dunn 19240

[Note: This is a MISSING PERSON REPORT contains info on Catherine's car, salary, employment, mental state, clothing, her physique, etc. Also "Gold wedding band Driver's license." Text in lower part says the following:]

Miss Phillips reports her roommate Catherine Cesnik left their apartment at 131 North Bend Rd on 7 Nov 69 7:30 PM to cash some checks at the Hecht Co 4501 Edmondson Ave. [Checks cannot be cashed at this department store.] Miss Phillips stated she has not seen or heard from Catherine since. Also, Miss Phillips could not give any reason for Miss Cesnik's disappearance, as she has never run away before. [Russell was in apartment the night before when student and her boyfriend came. Maskell and Magnus arrived soon after. Was Russ afraid of the police who were involved?]

08-Nov-69 4:40 AM Robert H. Becker (?) 2976 SW

Sgt. J.T. Dunn 19240: [in Box 5 "Date of Original Report" is written: 3 AM 8 Nov 69]. Father Peter McKeon a friend of Catherine Cesnik reports that he found her Ford Maverick parked of the 4500 Blk of Carriage Court, the car was unlocked and parked far from the curb. [Koob told Gemma they found the car together. Says he told Pete not to touch anything. Koob opened driver door. McKeon opened passenger door.]

08-Nov-69, 1:45 pm, James A. Jones 38128 [this would have been Saturday afternoon]

In reference to the vehicle driven by Miss Cesnick [sic], same was located by Mr. Peter McKeon in the 4500 Carriage Ct. at 4:00 AM 8 Nov 69 [above report says 3 am]. The vehicle a 1970 Ford Maverick Sedan. MD HG6341 was towed to the Southwestern Dist. by Varsity Towing and was processed by Offs John McClellan and Gary Jones from the crime laboratory. Inside of the vehicle was one Muhley's Bakery box contents unknown, one turned over litter basket, mud on the tires and branches on the windshield and on the interior of the car. [No mention of twig on turn signal] The car was entered by Mr. McKeon, when he found same. Off. Joseph Powell Homicide Squad was present when the car was processed.

[Missing page 3]

08-Nov-69 1:45 PM [Saturday afternoon]

D.E. James, A. Jones 38128

In company with Lt. Matarazza and Sgt. W. Holland we went to 131 D N.Bend Rd. and interviewed the following persons. Miss Russell Phillips FW-25 [female/white/25 years] 131 D North Bend Rd. Mr. Peter McKeon M-W-38 [male/white/38] Ammendale Beltsville MD and Mr. Gerard Koob M-W-31 Manresa Annapolis MD all close friends of the missing person. All of the persons that were interviewed report that Miss Cesnick [sic] left 131 D N. Bend Rd. on 7 Nov. 69 at 7:30 P.M. [Koob and McKeon would not know the time she left] enroute to the 1st National Bank, Catonsville Branch and to do some shopping at the Hecht Company and stop at Muhley's Bakery located at Frederick and Paradise Aves. [Muhley's is in the Hecht Company, not at Frederick and Paradise]

08-Nov-69 2:00 PM Joseph C. Weich (?) S.W. 81740James A. Jones 381287

In reference to the above missing person, I interviewed the following people in regard to the car, parked on the north west corner of Carriage Court and North Bend Rd. Due to the contiguous numbering of the courts, Lantern Court was an extension of Carriage Court. [Koob says car was on corner of Lantern Court, not Carriage Court. Because of the configuration of the courts, the car may have been more easily visible from the houses on Carriage Court. Old photo from *The Keepers* also shows car parked at Lantern Court] 1. Mrs. Diane Magersupp F-W-age 21 5308 Carriage Ct. phone xxxxxxx. Mrs. Magersupp stated she doesn't remember seeing the car last night; she saw it parked on the corner at 8:00 A.M. this morning, Nov. 8, 1969. [She would be seventy-one now.] 2. Mrs. Beulah Deitrick F-W-age 56 5306 Carriage Ct. phone xxx-xxxx. Mrs. Deitrick stated she does not know anything about the car. 3. Mr. William Donaldson stated he saw the car parked on the corner at 12:05 A.M. this date Nov. 8, 1969. [No contact info.] 4. Mrs. Patricia Mormann W-F- age 34 5307A Carriage Ct. phone xxx-xxxx stated she saw the car parked on the corner at 10:00 . Nov. 7, 1969. [She would be in her eighties. Earliest time seeing the car.] She did not see anyone around the car. 5. Miss Mary Brigerman F-W-age 40 5305A Carriage Ct phone xxx-xxxx. Miss Brigerman stated she saw the car parked on the corner at 11:00 P.M. Nov. 7, 1969. She did not see anyone around the car. 6. Mrs. Pat Cavero F-W-age 21 5301A Carriage Ct. phone xxx-xxxx Mrs. Cavero stated she saw the car parked on the corner at 11:00 P.M. She did not see anyone around the car. 7. Mrs. Mary Hallwig F-W-age - over 21 5300

Carriage CT. phone xxx-xxxx Mrs. Hallwig stated she did not know anything about the car. 8. Mrs. John W. Leonard W-M-age 68 5346 Jamestown Ct. phone xxx-xxxx Mr. Leonard is the resident manager of the Jamestown and Carriage Ct. apartments. He stated that he does not know anything about the car. 9. Mr. David Hutton W-M-age 24 5310 Carriage Ct. phone xxx-xxxx Mr. Hutton stated he saw the car parked on the corner at 11:30 P.M. Nov. 7, 1969. He did not see anyone around the car.

08-Nov-69 3:00 PM John Scales (?) 66995, Jack Smyala (?) Emergency Unit CP12

Off. Howard Lindsey Note: Address is "5200 Blk Frederick Ave" Correct Offense is "Area Search" Text is: 7. At request of Southwestern District, we assisted K-9 and District officers in search of wood area of North Bend, Frederick Road Negative Results

08-Nov-69 4:15 PM Sgt. L. Zeminsky (?) TAC 85780

Text: At 1:30 PM this date searched the area in the vicinity of the 200 Blk. Of N. Bend Rd for a missing W-F-26, one Catherine Cesnik, 131 N Bend Rd. The area was searched with 4 K-9 teams with negative results. Information was received from one Mrs. Betty Malcolm, W-F-40 yrs., 6326 Carriage Ct, she stated she observed a young W-M- wearing a light jacket park a dark colored car in the 5300 Blk of Carriage Ct at about 10 P.M. The youth walked south toward Frederick Av and she thought this unusual because there was ample room to park further down the street. [Edgar and friend Bobby Thompson both lived less than two miles straight down Frederick Road from Carriage House on Potter Street apartments.]

08-Nov-69 7:30 PM Sgt. Robert M Leftwich (?) Tac

In regard to the above missing person, Miss Catherine Ann Cesnik, W/F 26 yrs., of 131 North Bend Rd. Field searches by K-9 Units: 2130, 2132, 2133, 2134, and 2154 were conducted in the vicinity of the 5300 Blk Frederick Rd. and in Leakin Park from 4 this PM till after dark (5:40 PM). [Why start so late in the day? Leakin Park is quite a few miles from the site, but a lot of bodies show up there.] The result of the searches for Miss Cesnik were negative. The searches were conducted under the supervision of K-9 Sgt. Robert M. Leftwich.

The following Divisions were notified. Lt. Harry Knecht Communications Lt. Wallace Ritter Homicide Squad Miss. Brander Chief Battaglia's Office I was unable to contact anyone in the Public Information Office. Sgt. L. Sieminski from the Tactical Section was notified all the wooded area in vicinity will be searched.

[Missing pages 1 and 2]

James A. Jones 38128

On 9 Nov. 69 at about 11:00 A.M., one Erick St. Jahn M-W-17 2930 Frederick Ave. came to the Southwest Station and he asked to see the Lieutenant. Mr. St. Jahn had a conference with Lt. Matarazzo in reference to the missing person Miss Catherine Cesnik.

At 12:00 this date Mr. and Mrs. Joseph Cesnik, parents of the missing person Catherine Cesnik came to the Southwest Station and turned over to me two pictures of their daughter Catherine. The pictures were placed in the folder.

Sgt. Frank Retterlor (?) 63470

Relative to this offense at 11:45 PM 8 Nov. a surveillance of 131 North Bend Rd. revealed a late model Chevrolet MD registration xxx-xxx was cruising in the area of 131 North Bend Rd. The operator of this vehicle parked same on the street opposite 131 North Bend Rd and walked toward the 131 Apt. building. The operator was identified as Joseph Cletus Noone M-W-24 (DOB 2-16-45) of 306 Kingston Rd Mr. Noone stated that he was a "friend of the church" and a close friend of Sister Catherine Cesnick and Sister Russell Phillips, who reside at 131 North Bend Rd. This information verified by Sister Phillips. Upon being interviewed Mr. Noone stated that he stays at 306 Kingston Rd. in company with Phillip Esserwein M-W-25, Edward Carson M-W and a subject named Dave. [These guys are all friends of the nuns. Carson, Noone and David Zangrilli taught at Keough and rented this house together. Esserwein is a music person who wrote music for church services.] Dave's last name is unknown at this time. On 11/9/69 at 10:30 AM the investigation continued at 131 North Bend Rd. speaking with Sister Phillips relative to any word from Sister Catherine Cesnick [sic] and if she knew the four (4) subjects mentioned by Mr. Noone. Sister Phillips advised that no information had been received relative to the missing person. She stated that the four subjects mentioned had dinner at her apartment on Wednesday 29 October 69. Sister Phillips further advised that one Thomas Conway M-W-24-25 with a Chester PA address unknown stopped by the apt on 7 Nov 69 at about

7:30 PM and asked for Sister Catherine [this guy is cleared as he was a priest friend of Cathy's, who was in town with a friend and stopped in to see her] and left after being advised that she had gone on an errand. C.I.D. Det. Rose - Homicide notified of this information. Under the direction of Capt. Simon J. Avara, in company of Lt. Leslie Stickles (K-9-Unit) a search area was set up to cover the area between Athol Ave to the W. County Line from Edmondson Ave to the wooded areas south of Frederick Ave – [This covers the area from the shopping center to the nuns' apartment.] with negative results. Joseph Noone was advised that his name and the names of others mentioned would be turned over to C.I.D. Missing Persons so that statements can be obtained.

09-Nov-69 7:30 PM Off. E. Weichert 87680 SW

About 6:00 pm this date [Nov. 9, 1969] Mr. Joseph Cesnik, father of the above missing person, called the S.W. Sta. [station] and spoke with Sgt. Edward Weichert relating the below information. Same to be sent to Pittsburgh Police. Request the following be placed on teletype. Attention: Pittsburgh Pennsylvania Police Dept. Relative to a missing person from this city, [Balto. Md.] Complaint # 8K-13879. TT# HO 518, one Catherine Cesnik, W-F-26 yrs, 5-5, 115 lbs., thin build, blond hair, fair complexion, wearing aqua coat, Navy Blue Suit, yellow sweater, black shoes, [I was told there was a yellow thread in the car but not where it was found] missing from 131 North Bend Rd. Balto.

[Missing Page 1. Sounds like the Bake Shop at Hecht's interviewees].

Sgt. Anthony Sano 68700

7. Mr. Bernard Klein W–M–35 yrs. 17 Mardrew Rd phone # xxx-xxxx reports about 9:00 PM or 9:10 PM 7 Nov. 69. While walking in the area of his home which is in the area where Miss Cesnik's auto was located he was walking on Mardrew Rd toward North Bend Rd. about 40 ft. from North Bend Road he passed a white male 20-25 yrs about 6'1" 150 lbs. – 170 lbs. slender build dark hair and dark clothing. The left arm of the man was hanging as if it was limp and he made a stomping noise when he walked. As Mr. Klein passed the subject the subject went up a dead-end alley off of Mardrew Rd which goes behind the homes on North Bend Rd. Mr. Klein said he would be able to identify the subject if seen again. Mr. Klein stated he has never seen this subject in the area before this time. Request Copy be sent to Homicide Squad. [Never heard this. I cannot think of anybody who would walk this way.]

12-Nov-69, [an internal memo, undated except for some kind of processing stamp. Nothing but this text:] CL 69 11216-4 Off. Jones & McClellan responded to Southwestern Station to process & photograph a Ford Maverick Md. Lic. HG 63 41 in regard to a missing person Catherine Ann Cesnik, Car processed for latent prints with negative results & if pictures are needed two days advance notice is required. [This is the station where Scannell worked.]

Officer Floyd Rouzee 65377

We then went to 131 D North Bend where we spoke with Miss Russell Phillips, roommate of complainant Missing Person, who reported that the parents were packing the belongings of Catherine and was moving same out. An envelope was obtained from the father, Joseph Cesnik, of the missing person, with a Baltimore Post mark dated 8 Nov 69 P.M. with #54 on same. The envelope was addressed to Miss Marilyn Cesnik and was in Miss Catherine Cesnik's handwriting. A check was made with the Postal Inspectors where I spoke with Inspector Bock who stated that the envelope could have been mailed sometime after the last collection on Friday 7 Nov 69, and not picked up until sometime Saturday 8 Nov 69 and not cancelled until the P.M. on Saturday 8 Nov 69. The #54 on the post mark is the number of the machine used to cancel the stamp. Further stated the only way to trace the letter was to know where it was mailed from. Miss Phillips states that when she or Catherine mailed any letters they were usually mailed from the school, Western High, or on the way Miss Phillips further stated if the envelope was mailed on the way it would have been mailed by Julia Murray W/F 352 Marydell Rd whom Miss Cesnik drove to school every day. Unable to speak with Julia Murray as she is at school at this time. Miss Phillips further states that an airline Hostess Sue McDaniels of apt. 1A told her that she saw the car on the parking lot about 8:30 P.M. 7 Nov 69 but did not notice if Miss Cesnik was in same. [This is the same woman that we heard was carrying groceries in and out and said she saw Cathy in the car at 8:30]. Miss Sue McDaniels was not at home this date.

[Note that there is no reference to what is in the envelope, if anything. Russell also acting like she did not mail it.]

[Missing page 1]

In reference to above missing person on orders from Lt. Matarazzo, Shift Commander, Police woman Sharon Martin and I went to 352 Marydell Rd where we interviewed one Julia Murray W/F 16 who reported that on Friday 7 Nov 69 when Miss Cesnik picked her up to take her to the school several pieces of mail was on the dash of the auto and was not mailed by her was taken into the school by Miss Cesnik. Julia did not ride home with Miss Cesnik as she got out of school at 3 PM and Miss Cesnik never left before 4 PM. She further stated there is a mail pick up at Western High School but does not know the time. Unable to ascertain time of pick up. Policewoman Martin and I then went to 5326 Carriage Court the home of Mrs. Betty Malcolm W/F 40 who observed a young W/M park a dark car in the 5300 Blk of Carriage Ct about 10 PM 7 Nov 69. Mrs. Malcolm was shown 5 photos of W/M's. Mrs. Malcolm picked out the photo of xxxx [guy she picked out was already incarcerated] and stated that she could not positively identify his photo as the person she saw but he most closely resembles the person she saw. Further stated if she saw the person in real life she still would not be able to identify him. We then went to 17 Mardrew Rd where the same photos were shown to Mr. Bernard Klum, but he was unable to pick out anyone. However stated the subject he saw was crippled. In reference to the envelope still unable to ascertain where it was mailed from. The only mailbox that we could find in the vicinity of Western High School was at the intersection of Cold Spring + Newport, the last collection at this box on Friday is 5 P.M. and the next collection is on Saturday at 9:26 A.M. the collections in the P.M. on Saturdays are 12:50 P.M. + 4:10 P.M. The Mt. Washington Branch of the Post Office which services Western High School was contacted but would not be able to tell if a collection of mail is made inside the school until Monday when the supervisor would be there.

18-Nov-69 12:00 PM Det. Joseph R. Powell 61729

Sgt. Harry Bannon 2600 C.I.D. In continuing this investigation, Father Gerard Joseph Koob consented to and was given a Polygraph examination by Lt. Frank Grunder of said unit at 2:00 P.M. 17 November 1969 and the results were negative. Brother Peter McKeon was also given a Polygraph examination by Lt. Frank Grunder at 10:30 A.M. 18 November 1969 and the results were negative. [Polygraphs given on two separate days.]

The body of Catherine Cesnik was discovered January 3, 1970, in Baltimore County. Dr. Werner Spitz, Medical Examiner for Baltimore City ruled death by Homicide. The investigation is being conducted by the Baltimore County Police Dept. Detective Bureau and Baltimore City Police Dept. Homicide Unit.

[There are many discrepancies in these reports from what newspapers reported.]

TIMELINE: A. JOSEPH MASKELL AND CATHERINE CESNIK

1939

April 13: Anthony Joseph Maskell is born. His mother (born 1903) is the second wife of his father, Joseph Francis Maskell, who came from Newcastle West, Co. Limerick, Ireland in 1898 with his parents, Daniel and Hanna Meade Maskell. Hanna was from Abbeyfeale, Kerry. They arrived in New York and settled in Baltimore, MD.

Raised in Northeast Baltimore near Clifton Park.

1942

Maskell's sister Maureen is born.

Maskell's older half-brother, Tom (born 1924) graduates from City College.

(November 17: Cathy Cesnik was born in the Lawrenceville neighborhood of Pittsburgh, PA.)

1943

Maskell's older half-brother, Tom, serves in the army until 1944.

1945

Maskell starts first grade.

1946

Maskell's older half-brother, Tom, joins the police force and works there until he is shot in 1966 and forced to retire.

1947

April 13: Maskell's eighth birthday. Since childhood, Anthony Joseph Maskell seemed destined for the priesthood. His favorite childhood game was "Mass." In child-sized vestments his mother had sewn for him, Joe would gather neighborhood children into the family's basement, where he would dispense the body of Christ in the form of white Necco wafers.

His mother, Helen Maskell, was very intent on her son becoming a priest recalls childhood friend Bill Heim. "I always wondered if he was going to revolt at some point," Heim says. "But he never did."

When young Joe is old enough to join in sandlot baseball games, he dresses in black and takes his position of choice behind the plate, calling the balls and strikes. According to Maskell's childhood friend, Bill Heim, who was interviewed for article "God Only Knows", Maskell liked having the authority to say: "This is right; that's wrong."

Fall: Cathy Cesnik starts first grade. She attends St. Mary Assumption Roman Catholic Church and School in Lawrenceville, PA. The school was operated by the School Sisters of Notre Dame (SSND), a teaching order.

1952

William Keeler graduates (BA) from St. Charles Borromeo Seminary in Wynnewood, PA. He later earned another bachelor's degree from St. Charles Seminary at Overbrook in Philadelphia. He received both a licentiate in sacred theology and a doctorate in canon law from Pontifical Gregorian University in Rome.

1953

April 13: Maskell's fourteenth birthday. At fourteen, Maskell goes to St. Charles Seminary in Catonsville, but returns after about a week because he is homesick.

Maskell starts his freshman year at Calvert Hall College High School

1954

April 13: Maskell's fifteenth birthday. Heim recalls that a fastidiously clean kid, a teenaged Maskell one year spent so much time immersed in his bathtub ritual that his father announced his displeasure over it. Joseph Francis Maskell, an office-furniture salesman with Lucas Brothers, was known for his short fuse.

1955

William Keeler ordained.

1956

April 13: Maskell's seventeenth birthday. According to Maskell's sister, Maureen Baldwin, he was so intent on becoming a priest that he never had a date in his life. When a girl he knew in high school told him he had the most beautiful eyes she had ever seen, he had no idea how to respond.

Friends from his teen years can't recall Maskell ever expressing a libido. "I never saw him with a girl the whole time we were in school," says Dennis Rogers, "outside of his mother."

Maskell starts his senior year at Calvert Hall College High School (when it was located downtown).

1957

Approximate: Maskell graduates from Calvert Hall College High School. The original school building was in downtown Baltimore where the AOB building is now.

Summer: According to a comment by Maskell survivor Patrick Forestell in 2015: "Maskell was a teenager attending St. Mary's Seminary in Roland Park in Baltimore. He and his friend, William Simms, were both teenage camp counselors at Saint Martin's Camp in Love Point, MD (Kent County), a summer camp for children from the St. Martin's Parish on Fulton Ave. in Baltimore. Maskell and Simms were allowed to become ordained, and they both inflicted harm on numerous children under the protection of the Archdiocese of Baltimore. Maskell used his superior IQ and manipulation to get what he wanted. At Saint Martin's Camp in 1957, William Simms was playing strip poker with the children in a cabin. Patrick was eleven years old, and a young, innocent child. Maskell was outside the cabin and lured him into the open area shower where he assaulted Patrick. Forestell says that his purpose in sharing this story is to show the hypocrisy of the Archdiocese of Baltimore for teaching theology to the masses while allowing monsters to exhibit evil deeds on numerous children over decades.

1958

April 13: Maskell's nineteenth birthday.

Maskell begins his first year at St. Mary's Seminary in Roland Park. When he tried seminary again, after high school, he liked it fine, and reveled in the privileges that came with being a third-year sacristan, which included free social time after Mass while the congregation prayed. The perks seemed to appeal to his ego. "He used to say with a smile, 'We're sacristans. It is our place to be back here'," recalls long-time friend and fellow seminarian William Kern.

Cathy Cesnik starts her junior year at St. Augustine High School. In high school, Cathy contemplated entering the religious life.

1959

Pope John XXIII announces the creation of the Second Vatican Council (also known as Vatican II) in January 1959. It shocks the world. There hasn't been an ecumenical council (an assembly of Roman Catholic religious leaders meant to settle doctrinal issues) in nearly 100 years.

1960

Spring: Cathy Cesnik graduates from St. Augustine High School. After graduation, Cathy moved to Baltimore to enter the Baltimore Province of the SSND in 1960 and took final vows on July 21, 1967.

Maskell ends his second year at St. Mary's Seminary.

1962

The Second Vatican Council is called (between 2,000 and 2,500 bishops and thousands of observers, auditors, sisters, laymen and laywomen) to four sessions at St. Peter's Basilica between 1962 and 1965. Sixteen documents came out of it, laying a foundation for the church as we know it today. William Keeler was a special adviser at the Second Vatican Council in the early 1960s.

1963

Maskell's father passes away at the age of sixty-seven.

1964

Christmas Eve: Maskell's half-brother sustains gunshot wounds that end his police career.

1965

Maskell is ordained.

Once ordained, Maskell is known for delivering thoughtful homilies with a compelling bass voice, and for excelling in the heroic moment. When Holy Cross parishioner Lynn Gerber Smith gave birth to an ailing baby, Maskell rushes to the hospital and performs an emergency baptism. When Maskell's friend Albert Griffith called to say he was depressed and thinking of "blowing my brains out," Maskell drives to Severna Park within fifteen minutes.

Maskell serves at Sacred Heart of Mary from 1965 to 1966.

Fall: Keough opens. As enrollment at all Catholic high schools increased, by the mid-1960s it becomes evident a new school is needed on the southwest side of the city. The School Sisters of Notre Dame respond to this need, and in 1965, Sr. Mary Virginia Connolly becomes the founding principal of Archbishop Keough High School. The school is built on thirty acres of land on Caton Avenue and is structured as an archdiocesan high school. Archbishop Keough High added one grade a year; the first commencement taking place in June 1969. The school flourishes, and in 1987 it is named an exemplary school by the U.S. Department of Education.

Cathy Cesnik begins her teaching career at Archbishop Keough High School on Caton Avenue (renamed Seton-Keough) when the school opens its doors in 1965. She teaches English literature and oversees the school's drama club. She is an energetic, enthusiastic and dedicated teacher. She is supportive and alert to her students at the all-girls school. (Taken from Cathy's obituary at findagrave.com).

In this year, Cathy moves into the residences for nuns at Keough.

1966

Sixteen months after his ordination, Maskell (now twenty-seven) becomes associate pastor at St. Clement in Lansdowne.

Teresa Harris Lancaster (Jane Roe) starts her freshman year at Keough.

Summer: Between seventh and eighth grade, Maskell survivor featured in *The Keepers* Charles Franz is an altar boy at Masses, where Charles gets to know Maskell.

Fall: Second year commences for Keough. New freshmen enter. Last year's students move up to sophomore. Cathy is still living in the convent at Keough.

Cathy meets Gerry Koob when he is an intern at Keough. Koob told *The Sun* that he and Cathy were deeply in love but that "it was a love between two celibates in a commitment to Christ." Koob described Cathy as a naive, unworldly young woman who had no sense of her own beauty or its effect on others.

Charles Franz starts eighth grade.

Maskell is giving Charles Franz rides home from Mass. Maskell would put the bike in the trunk, and they'd stop for a Snowball. Father Maskell regularly comes into Charles Franz' classroom saying he wants to see Charles at the rectory. At first it is once a week. Then it is 2 or 3 times per week. Often Maskell would keep Charles from lunch until the day ended (2:30). Maskell taught Charles how to drink and take drugs to forget what was happening around him. Maskell would call Charles Franz (thirteen) out of class at the parish school to chat, usually for several hours at a time, two or three times a week. They often start out talking about sports, but invariably the subject shifts to male anatomy.

One day, Maskell took Charles and two other boys target shooting. On the drive home, Charles sat up front with Maskell, and as the car rose over a bump in the road, Charles alleges, Maskell reached over, grabbed Charles's crotch, and said playfully, "Hold on to your balls."

1967

Maskell serves at St. Clement.

Maskell also serves as a chaplain for the Maryland State Police and Baltimore County Police and Maryland National Guard and later the Air National Guard as a Lieutenant colonel. (Dates unknown).

In *The Keepers*, Charles says that in May of 1967, his mother went downtown to the Archdiocese and went straight to the top and said, "Father Maskell is abusing my eighth-grade son." Maskell was then assigned to Archbishop Keough High School for girls.

July 21: Cathy takes final vows. Her professed name is Sister Joanita.

Fall: Maskell survivors Jean Hargadon and Lil Hughes start their freshman year at Keough. Charles starts his freshman year at Mt. St. Joseph High School.

This is the third year Keough has been open. This is the start of Maskell's first year as school chaplain and counselor at Keough. Cathy starts her third year teaching at Keough. She is still living in the convent at Keough.

1968

Maskell has limited duties at St. Clement and also serves at Our Lady of Victory.

Old St. Clement rectory is sold to the Garmer family. Maskell moves to the rectory at Our Lady of Victory parish while new rectory is being built.

April 6–14: Baltimore riots.

Cathy completes her third year teaching at Keough.

1969

John A. "Pete" McKeon, a Christian brother, meets Cathy Cesnik and Gerry Koob at a retreat for Notre Dame sisters in Boston.

March 31: Ford's new Maverick becomes available for sale for approximately $2,000.00. Cathy would have purchased this car sometime between April and October of 1969. It has been reported that Cathy and Russ jointly purchased the vehicle and shared it. At some point, police returned the Maverick to Russ, who continued to drive it after Cathy's death.

May: Jean confides in Cathy that a priest had sexually abused her at Keough.

Spring of 1969 is the end of Cathy's fourth year teaching at Keough. Cathy and Russell ask for permission to live outside the forty-sister convent but to continue teaching as nuns, but outside of Archbishop Keough.

June: Russell and Cathy leave Keough (and the residence), adopt civilian dress, get teaching jobs in city schools, and move into the Carriage House Apartments on North Bend Road, in Southwest Baltimore.

June 1, 1969: Letter from Cathy explains her decision to leave Keough.

November 7: Cathy disappears.

1970

January 3: Cathy's body is found by hunter George Brown and his stepson.

2017

May 19: *The Keepers* is released on Netflix.

2019

November 7: Fifty-year anniversary of Cathy Cesnik's disappearance.

2020

As of the date of this book's writing, the case remains unsolved.

TIMELINE OF ASSIGNMENTS
FOR A. JOSEPH MASKELL

DATE	SOURCE OF INFO	EVENT	DISCUSSION
April 13, 1939	*God Only Knows*, death certificate, ancestry.com family tree	Date of birth	Raised by parents in NE Baltimore. Half-brother, Tommy. Mother, S. Helen Jenkins. Father, Joseph Francis Maskell. Sister, Maureen M. Baldwin.
~1953	*God Only Knows*	Entered St. Charles Seminary for one week.	Age 14, got homesick and returned home.
~1956 – 1957		Graduated from Calvert Hall College High School.	
~1957	*God Only Knows*, news story with ordination of William Simms	Entered St. Mary's Seminary.	Newspaper story about ordination of William Simms says Joseph Maskell was acolyte, seminarian from St. Mary's Seminary Roland Park.
1965	Maskell's tombstone	Ordained	
1965 – 1966	Baltimore List of Clergy accused of child sexual abuse [Called "List"]	Assigned to Sacred Heart of Mary.	
1966 – 1968	List, *God Only Knows*	Associate pastor at St. Clement Church in 1966. Supervised Boy Scouts there.	Multiple reports of abuse.
December 24, 1968	News Stories	Baltimore City Policeman, half-brother Joseph T. Maskell (Tommy) shot while on duty, survives.	

1968 – 1970	List	Living at Our Lady of Victory rectory while serving as AKHS chaplain.	Several reports of abuse.
1967 – 1975	*God Only Knows*	Chaplain at Archbishop Keough High School.	Multiple reports of abuse by priests, police officers, politicians and businesspersons.
November 4, 1969	Land records	Old St. Clement rectory sold to Garmer family.	St. Clement built new rectory and sold old one.
November 7, 1969	News stories	Sister Cathy last seen/abducted one day after Maskell and Magnus visited at apartment.	Keough victim and boyfriend there with Cathy and Russell when Maskell/Magnus arrived.
November 11, 1969	News stories	Joyce Malecki abducted/ murdered.	Joyce was parishioner at St. Clement, knew Maskell from retreats. Body found on Fort Meade property.
November 1969			Jane Doe states Maskell took her to see Cathy's body.
January 3, 1970	News stories. Podcast *Foul Play* interview with hunter		Sister Cathy's body found by two hunters.
1972	News story	Maskell earned master's degree in school psychology from Towson State University and then certificate of advanced study in counseling from the Johns Hopkins University.	No evidence of degree in pharmacology, gynecology.
1975		Removed from Keough and assigned to AOB Division of Schools.	

1975 – 1980	AOB assignment list	Lived and assisted at St. Clement while at the Division of Schools. Address: Archdiocese Of Baltimore Division Of Catholic Schools 320 Cathedral Street Baltimore, Maryland 21201.	Alleged to have gone before AOB tribunal. Alleged to have been evaluating foster children for placement by Catholic Charities organization affiliated with the AOB.
1980 – 1982	List	Served at Annunciation.	Allegations of abuse of young boys who were on baseball team.
1982 – Oct 1992		Pastor of Holy Cross parish.	Buried documents in cemetery in 1990. Alleged relationship with girl at HC starting at age 16 until 22. Police report from 1989: family alleged their mother's body not buried in designated plot. Lived at "Priest's House" in Federal Hill. Housekeeper alleges cleaning up pornography from several of the priests living there.
1990	News story	Buried documents in Holy Cross cemetery.	Multiple pickup truck loads of boxes; Mr. Storey (caretaker) reportedly took some incriminating documents and used them to blackmail Maskell.
Jan 1991	News story	Mr. Storey fired from Holy Cross by Maskell on Christmas Eve.	

October 1992 to ~ April 1993		Psychiatric hospital in Connecticut for just under six months.	Confronted by archdiocese in Oct 1992 after allegations from Doe/Roe, sent to psych hospital in Connecticut, The Institute for Living. After evaluation, deemed "able to return to ministry."
Jan 10, 1993	Land records	Mother, Helen Maskell, died.	Maskell handled selling of her home. Blamed her death on scandal.
~ April 1993	Newspaper stories, God Only Knows.	Back from CT., assigned to administrative post at St. Augustine's parish.	AOB not willing to put Maskell in parish setting. Maskell hired canon lawyer to defend himself. Said, with no proof of abuse, AOB had no legal right to refuse to assign him to parish. Protests at St. Augustine's.
March 18, 1994	Land records	Sale of deceased mother's home closes (he is personal representative for estate in sale).	Buyer reported seeing home contents in dumpster, with hoard of cash inside of TV.
December 1994	News story	Cemetery pit contents removed; Holy Cross church is in Baltimore City, but cemetery is in Anne Arundel County.	Mr. Storey contacted Baltimore City police after publicity about Doe/Roe, led them to site. Documents taken by City police. Assistant State's Attorney Sharon May present.
August 1994	God Only Knows, newspaper stories, Justice Facebook discussion by posters.	Returned to Institute for Living at his request.	

1994	List	Placed on administrative leave.	
August 3, 1994	News stories		Maskell resigned from the Air Guard and was assigned to the Inactive Ready Reserve, according to public information officer. Maskell had been senior chaplain of the 135th Air Transport Group, based at Martin State Airport. Removed from advisory board of Operation Challenge, guard-sponsored program for high school dropouts at Aberdeen Proving Ground.
~ Oct 1995	*God Only Knows*	Lived with Robert Hawkins, pastor of St. Rita's, for several weeks (exact dates unknown).	Stayed with Hawkins, then fled to Ireland. Baltimore Archbishop had inquiry from Ireland as Maskell applied to join priest order there. No extradition treaty with Ireland. Maskell asked to return to Institute for Living.
May 1995			Doe/Roe vs. Maskell motion trial.
1995		Paul Mandelbaum's "God Only Knows" published in *Baltimore Magazine*.	
September 1995	Court documents	On appeal, Baltimore City court decision that Doe/Roe versus Maskell case could not go to trial because of SOL was upheld.	Case never went to trial; hearing on motion to dismiss was approved.

Unknown to 2001	SNAP records	Returned from Ireland to US. Lived at Little Sisters of the Poor in Catonsville until stroke: transferred to Stella Maris nursing home in Towson.	Survivor Lil Hughes visited at Stella Maris and confirmed he was there, wheelchair bound and disorientated.
May 7, 2001	Social Security death index, death certificate	Died at St. Joseph Hospital disabled from stroke. Cause of death: bilateral pneumonia, decompensated heart failure, and myocardial infarction [heart attack].	Buried in Holy Family cemetery in Baltimore County with parents.
February 2018	News reports	Maskell's body exhumed for complete DNA profile.	

About the Author

Gemma Staub Hoskins is a native of Baltimore, Maryland. She is a product of the Archdiocese of Baltimore Catholic Schools system, attending Saint William of York parochial school and Archbishop Keough High School. A graduate of Towson State University, Hoskins was an elementary teacher for twenty-six years. Hoskins also holds a master's degree in Instructional Technology and advanced certificates in Staff Development and Facilitative Leadership.

Gemma Hoskins was named the 1992 Maryland Teacher of the Year. Her career spans forty years, during which time she was also a teacher mentor and professional development specialist for Harford and Baltimore County Public Schools. She has taught adult learners and provided professional development for mentors and teachers throughout Maryland. She has written and developed curriculum and assessment at local and state levels. Hoskins' career in education includes travel and presentations in New Zealand and Russia, as well as Alabama, Virginia, and Tennessee. Gemma Hoskins is published in the 1995 edition of *Educational Psychology* by Dr. Robert Slavin, PhD. Gemma was married to the late Ernest Joseph Hoskins, who died of cancer in 1989. She is featured as a grassroots investigator in the Netflix series *The Keepers*. Hoskins now resides on the Eastern Shore of Maryland with her loyal dog, Teddy, where she paints, writes and continues to pursue justice for Sister Cathy Cesnik and Joyce Malecki, and survivors of clergy abuse around the globe. She can be heard weekly on the podcast *Foul Play*, where she and her cohost, Shane Waters, delve into unsolved crimes and the lives of individuals impacted by those acts.